D.E.A.P.

Drop Everything and Pray

D.E.A.P.

Drop Everything And Pray

A Daily Scripture, Prayer and Song Suggestion

Suzi Corrigan Ullmann

INTRODUCTION

Does God talk to people? I thought if God talked to anyone it would be a church leader, someone important or someone who spent hours in a church. I never thought that God would talk to me, a mom, a wife, a teacher – just a 'normal' person. But He did and here is my story:

I spent more than half my life not knowing that God 'talks to' people. I attended Catholic schools from kindergarten through high school. I have always believed in the Father, Son/Jesus, and Holy Spirit. I went to church regularly. Following college, I became a special education teacher, and got married. God granted my wishes for having children, 2 sons. I assumed I knew everything I needed to know about God and about life in general. In 1994, my husband, Steve, and I had just started the process of building the all-American dream house. We signed legal commitments and placed a hefty deposit on the dream house, but something deep inside me felt unsettled, an inarticulate "knowing" that I was not to buy this house. Steve confided that he felt the same 'knowing'. We had no reasons, no explanations for our feelings. Finally, we agreed that "God does not want us to buy this house" and we canceled the contract.

At this time our older son was four years old, our younger son just one. We bought a different house and the week before we planned to move in, we were devastated to learn that our oldest son was diagnosed with leukemia. In that moment, Steve and I knew that God was looking out for us. There is no way that we could have afforded the dream house due to my 3+ years' leave of absence from work. In addition, our new home was much closer to the hospital than the dream house. God's communication started to make sense.

While in the depths of 3 1/2 years of chemotherapy, my fervent prayer was to let my son live to take his First Communion. Of course, I prayed that my son would become cancer free and live a full life as well. I started walking and running trying to cope with the demands of having a one-year-old and a steroid-crazed 4-year-old battling cancer. On a walk where I was crying out to a silent God, I 'heard' from Him again. It was a similar experience, a 'knowing'- not an audible voice but more like an audible thought. "You are going to be OK; I am taking care of you." From then on, although I still had bouts of fear and anxiety, I knew that no matter what happened, God was with me. God did not tell me that my son would be all right, but that I would be all right - no matter what. My whole outlook changed, and I was able to carry the burdens knowing, really knowing, that God was carrying me. As I write this, my son is 30 years cancer free!!

God has continued to 'talk' or communicate with me over the years in different ways. I have had many experiences, too numerous to share. It astonishes me that I lived so long with such limited knowledge of God and of God's ways. It is one of the reasons that I wanted to write this book: so that others can learn earlier what took me so long to learn and experience. I hope that this book will guide You to facilitate a deeper relationship with Your Father. I hope that You will allow God's peace, love, joy and hope to fill you and strengthen You as You grow closer to Him. This is my prayer for you!

A NOTE FROM THE AUTHOR

(Helpful Tips to Get the Most Out of this Book)

I hope this devotional guides you in your quest for a deeper, richer relationship with God. With all my heart, I want you to know the God I have experienced: The God Who communicates with you; The God Who cares about You in every way; The God Who is sovereign and holy and fearsome in power, yet gentle and compassionate; The God Who loves You without condition; The God Who knows and wants what is best for you.

I believe the greatest benefits to you will come from your faithful, habitual time using this daily book. I hope it will help you to: Discover the value of your time with God; Learn from the scriptures who God is and what following Him means; Nurture an intimate relationship so that you can talk with God daily and share your passions resulting in a more positive way of life.

It is important to note that your journey toward a dynamic, mature life with God will challenge your will and take so much longer than you can imagine. Expect ups and downs, and course corrections, but the good news is that we have a patient God who is cheering you on.

How can you maximize your efforts? Try taking charge of your environment. Slow down, prepare a place for Him. Find a quiet, comfortable space where you can be alone, without noise or interruption. Each time that You meet with God, be intentional about seeking, listening, praising, during your prayer time. Create an environment where You are open to spiritual communication. Let your inhibitions go, and visualize God, Jesus and the Holy Spirit sitting with you in your prayer space. Imagine His light, His peace, His love surrounding you.

If you are rushed, you will not receive the full benefits of your prayer time. I suggest reading the scripture of the day at least twice to make sure you grasp the intent. Remember, you can ask God to help you understand! Take time to let God communicate how this scripture might relate to your life right now. Think about how this scripture might apply directly to you.

Keep in mind that the prayer is not written to be read; it is written for you to pray it. Read one line or one phrase at a time. Pause, take a breath at commas and periods. You can stop and communicate your personal thoughts with God at any time. You can repeat sentences and phrases as you wish. Personalize the prayer as much as you want. After all, it is your time to communicate your thoughts, feelings, needs, and requests.

To get the most benefit from your prayer experience, schedule your prayer time like any other cannot miss appointment. Be consistent, diligent. When I began carving out time to pray, I worked a full-time job, cared for my two children, and volunteered in my church and community. The only way to pray regularly was to schedule praying time early in the morning and for me, this practice has truly been a life changing gift.

I've added a song title and artist so you can google and listen to the song if you like. Each song is as close to the daily theme as I could find. You may choose to listen to the song during your morning prayer time or listen on your phone later in the day. I love music and these songs inspire me in deep and meaningful ways, so I hope you, too, find the songs helpful and enjoyable along your journey.

This devotional is written so that you have a prayer for each day. I have devised the layout so that there are 31 common themes, one theme written on the same number day of the month. See Table of Contents for specific themes. (For example, the first of every month focuses on knowing that our God is sovereign and holy, the fifteenth of each month focuses on the Presence of God). I have organized the devotional this way intentionally so that if you have an area where you feel that you need support, then you can easily find scriptures and prayers in that area and you can spend time with God using these pages to guide you and help you. For example, if you are having difficulty with anxiety, you can go to the 19th of every month and focus on those scriptures and prayers. My hope is that you use this book to guide you in whatever way will be most beneficial to you!

TABLE OF CONTENTS

26th of every month .... Perseverance
27th of every month .... I am a Child of God
28th of every month .... Motivation
29th of every month .... Pray for Others
30th of every month: .... I Am......
31st of every month: .... I Will......

Holy, Sovereign God

Yours, O Lord, is the greatness and the power and the glory and the victory and the majesty, for all that is in the heavens and the earth is Yours; Yours is the kingdom, O Lord, and Yours it is to be exalted as Head overall.

1 Chronicles 29:11 (Amplified Bible-Amp)

Father God,

I start this new year with a purpose to get to know You more. As I read and think about this scripture, I see that You have all power, all glory, all victory. You have dominion over all things. I take this in as I quiet myself in Your Presence right now. I ask You to give me knowledge and understanding of You today and all year long. I acknowledge that You are the one true and holy Lord. I pray not only for knowledge, but I pray that I will continue to deepen my relationship with You. I look forward to spending this special prayer time with You, experiencing You, knowing You more and more. I look forward to increased love, joy, peace, grace, confidence, and hope as I spend time with You each day. I envision myself being wrapped in Your arms, in Your love as I spend this time in prayer with You. I am so grateful that as holy and sovereign and powerful as You are, that You would want to spend time with me. I am gratefully Yours. I pray this in Jesus' name.

Song Suggestion: Majesty (Here I am) *by* Promise Keepers

Praise

Praise the LORD! Praise God in His sanctuary; praise Him in His mighty firmament! Praise Him for his mighty acts; praise Him according to His excellent greatness! Praise Him with the sound of the trumpet; praise Him with the lute and harp! Praise Him with the timbrel and dance; praise Him with stringed instruments and flutes! Praise Him with loud cymbals; praise Him with clashing cymbals! Let everything that has breath praise the LORD. Praise the LORD!

Psalm 150:1-6 (New King James Version-NKJV)

Father God,

This morning, I start my day praising You! I choose to spend time thinking about how good You are, how good You have been to me. Even if circumstances in my life are not perfect, I can still say that You are good; You are worthy to be praised. Even as this world seems more and more chaotic, stressful, and troublesome, you are still on the throne in the heavens breathing life into all, working with me for my good. I thank You Lord and I praise you now. Help me to remember to take time throughout this day to praise You for Your goodness. I pray this prayer in Jesus' name.

Song Suggestion: Everything That Has Breath (Praise) *by* Jesus Culture, Bryan and Katie Torwalt

January 3

Wisdom

If any of you is deficient in wisdom, let him ask of the giving God [Who gives] to everyone liberally and ungrudgingly, without reproaching or faultfinding, and it will be given him. Only it must be in faith that he asks with no wavering (no hesitating, no doubting). For the one who wavers (hesitates, doubts) is like the billowing surge out at sea that is blown hither and thither and tossed by the wind.

James 1:5-6 (Amp)

Father God,

I need You! I need Your help to live in a way that is honoring and pleasing to You. I cannot do it on my own. So, I humbly ask You to give me wisdom - open my eyes and my ears, my heart and my mind so I can think the way you want me to think, to say what you would want me to say (or when to keep quiet) and do what you would want me to do. Your Word says that I can ask, and You will give Your wisdom to me freely if I believe. And so, I thank You now because I believe You are helping me and will continue to work with me so I can be all You have made me to be. I pray this in Jesus' name.

Song Suggestion: God, I Look to You *by* Jenn Johnson

Forgiven

Wrongdoings prevail against me; as for our offenses, You forgive them.

Psalm 65:3 (New American Standard Bible-NASB)

Father God,

I am filled with gratitude and awe that You are such a merciful and forgiving God. You know my every flaw, my weaknesses, each one of my sins. I am sorry for sinning against You. I am sorry for the times I did not do what I knew was right. Yet You still love me and watch over me and You forgive me repeatedly. I start this day with Your grace and mercy filling me. I accept these free gifts with open arms. I will do my best to purposefully live this day remembering that I am forgiven and loved completely by You. With gratitude, I pray in Jesus' name.

Song Suggestion: Grace Like Rain *by* Todd Agnew

Open Ears

"He who has an ear, let him hear what the Spirit says to the churches."

Revelation 3:22 (NKJV)

Father God,

You speak in many ways - through others, through church leaders, through music and especially through Your Word, the Bible. I ask You to ignite a passion in me to get to know you through Your Word. Open my ears to hear and help me to learn. Change me from the inside out. I ask You to open my ears and my heart to You today and all though this new year. I ask this in Jesus' name.

Song Suggestion: From the Inside Out *by* Phillips, Craig, and Dean

Joy

Be happy [in your faith] and rejoice and be glad hearted continually (always); Be unceasing in prayer [praying perseveringly]; Thank [God] in everything [no matter what the circumstances may be, be thankful and give thanks], for this is the will of God for you [who are] in Christ Jesus [the Revealer and Mediator of that will].

1 Thessalonians 5:16-18 (Amp)

Father God,

Thank You for wanting me to be filled with joy. Thank You that You know best, and You want what is best for me. This scripture (Your Word) is teaching me to be thankful no matter what is going on around me and to be persistent in prayer. I ask the Holy Spirit to remind me each day to look for reasons to be joyful and thankful and then I will send my thanks to You all day long. The more I think about You and all Your blessings, the more joy I have. I am rejoicing in You right now, in this very moment Father, because of all the love that you are pouring out on me. I pray this prayer with joy and gratitude in Jesus' name.

Song Suggestion: Joy *by* for King and Country

January 7

Love God, Love Others

"Teacher, which is the great commandment in the law?" Jesus said to him, "'You shall love the LORD your God with all your heart, with all your soul, and with all your mind.' "This is the first and great commandment, "And the second is like it: 'You shall love your neighbor as yourself.' On these two commandments hang all the Law and the Prophets."

Matthew 22:36-40 (NKJV)

Father God,

Thank You for guiding me on this journey with You. I am learning more and more to love You, with my whole heart, soul, and mind. You are my only God. Please, please continue to teach me and lead me on this journey. I need Your Spirit to continue to teach and guide me when it comes to loving others in the way You want me to. Help me put others' needs before my own, to really listen attentively to others, to take time (even when it is inconvenient) for others, help me be willing to be interrupted to help other people, and to give of myself (my time, my attention, my "things", my money). I am trusting You to help me change. I praise You and want to please You every day. I pray this prayer in Jesus' name.

Song Suggestion: Love God Love People *by* Danny Gokey

Names of God

El Shaddai

In Hebrew this means: God is the all sufficient One; He gives life; He nurtures; He pours out blessings.

When Abram was ninety-nine years old, the LORD appeared to him and said, "I am El-Shaddai- 'God Almighty.' Serve me faithfully and live a blameless life. I will make a covenant with you, by which I will guarantee to give you countless descendants."

Genesis 17:12 (NLT)

Father God,

I believe that You are the ONE Almighty God. You are El Shaddai, the One who is all sufficient. You give life, You give me life. You pour out Your blessings on me. You nurture me and You are all I need. Thank You for all that You are. Thank You for all You are doing for me, have already done and what You are going to do in the future. Help me be more aware of Your Presence. Help me remember who You are - El Shaddai, the all sufficient God. And help me to live my life in a way to honor who You are. In Jesus' name I pray.

Song Suggestion: El Shaddai *by* Amy Grant

Jesus

Jesus replied, I am the Bread of Life. He who comes to Me will never be hungry, and he who believes in and cleaves to and trusts in and relies on Me will never thirst any more (at any time).

John 6:35 (Amp)

Jesus,

I believe in You. I believe all that You spoke while You were here on Earth. I believe You are the Bread of Life. I believe You are all I need. I am so thankful that You fill my heart and soul with all I need. I am so thankful to You for showing me a better way to live.

Help me to remember that I can always come to You. I trust in You as I place my whole self in Your arms. I trust that You will meet my needs and spiritually fill me. I will always praise You and thank You. I praise You and thank You right now in this quiet moment. In all quiet moments, I take You into my heart. In Jesus' name I pray.

Song Suggestion: I Am the Bread of Life *by* Jamie Lowthian

Eternity Minded

He will swallow up death [in victory; He will abolish death forever]. And the Lord God will wipe away tears from all faces; and the reproach of His people He will take away from off all the earth; for the Lord has spoken it.

Isaiah 25:8 (Amp)

Father God,

I push away all my worries and thoughts about all momentary circumstances in my life. I am replacing all these anxieties with Your promises about my future. You God, take away death forever and replace it with life. A life in which You, my Father, will wipe away all regrets, all shame, every sorrow, and pain. You take away all I am ashamed of. You give me each breath while I am here on earth, and You will give me a beautiful life for eternity. There is no way to repay You for such gifts. But with all I am, I give You my gratitude and love. In Jesus' saving name I pray today.

Song Suggestion: There Will Come a Day *by* Faith Hill

January 11

Believing

"For God so loved the world, that He gave His only Son, so that everyone who believes in Him will not perish, but have eternal life. For God did not send the Son into the world to judge the world, but so that the world might be saved through Him.

John 3:16-17 (New American Standard Bible - NASB)

God, my Father,

I believe in You. I believe You sent Jesus to show Your deep, all-encompassing love. I believe Jesus did Your will while He was on the earth. He willingly gave up His own royalty, His own majesty and allowed Himself to become the payment, the sacrifice for my sins. I believe Jesus took my sins to the cross and suffered horrendous pain and suffering on every level - He was tortured, and He died. I believe, Jesus, that You suffered and died for me. I believe You rose from the dead on that third day. I believe You are my Savior. I now live for you, not to earn my salvation but to please You and show my gratitude for all You have done for me. I gratefully pray this prayer today in Your Son, Jesus' name.

Song Suggestion: God So Loved *by* We the Kingdom

January 12

Peace

Peace I leave with you; My [own] peace I now give and bequeath to you. Not as the world gives do I give to you. Do not let your hearts be troubled, neither let them be afraid. [Stop allowing yourselves to be agitated and disturbed; and do not permit yourselves to be fearful and intimidated and cowardly and unsettled.]

John 14:27 (Amp)

Jesus,

You have given me Your perfect peace. I thank You for Your peace. I quiet myself now in Your Presence. I meditate on Your peace. I breathe it in and take it into me. My mind, my soul, my body is refreshed. I rejoice in You and the peace which You give me. Help me remember that Your peace is within me. Always. I just need to lean into Your Presence and let Your peace calm me and give me tranquility, courage, and strength.

Thank You for Your peace and love. In Jesus' name I pray.

Song Suggestion: Peace Be Still *by* Hope Darst

God's Will

He has showed you, O man, what is good. And what does the Lord require of you but to do justly, and to love kindness and mercy, and to humble yourself and walk humbly with your God?

Micah 6:8 (Amp)

Father God,

Thank you for Your Word which helps me navigate my thoughts and my actions. You are so clear, and Your ways are perfect. I ask You this morning to help me do Your good and perfect will. Help me live every day by treating everyone I meet justly and with love, compassion, and kindness. Holy Spirit, remind me to smile, to listen, to be giving, to use my words only to encourage and lift others up. Help me to remember that I am the receiver of all Your goodness, compassion, kindness, and mercy. May that inspire me and move me to do Your will today and for all my days. I ask You to encourage me to walk humbly with You each and every one of my days. Thank You, thank You Father, for this opportunity. With praise and thanksgiving, I pray this prayer in Jesus' holy name.

Song Suggestion: Act Justly, Love Mercy, Walk Humbly *by* Pat Barrett

January 14

Thoughts/Mindset

[Inasmuch as we] refute arguments and theories and reasonings and every proud and lofty thing that sets itself up against the [true] knowledge of God; and we lead every thought and purpose away captive into the obedience of Christ (the Messiah, the Anointed One),

2 Corinthians 10:5 (Amp)

Father God,

This morning, I am thinking about my thoughts. As You already know, my thoughts are not consistently centered on You. I don't even fully realize that I can control my thoughts in any way. BUT YOU SAY I CAN. So, this is an area where I need Your Holy Spirit to guide me and help me. Help me to take my thoughts and redirect them so that they are thoughts of mercy, grace, goodness, kindness, and Your truth. Oh, this will take a lot of work on Your part and mine! Give me persistence to keep working on this while the Holy Spirit is working alongside me! This seems like an infinite task, but I believe Your way is best, and I believe You are working with me. I am so grateful to have an ever-present guide. Thank You for helping me have the best life possible! Thank You, Father, Spirit, Jesus. I pray in Jesus' name.

Song Suggestion: Mind of Christ *by* Natalia Chase

January 15

The Presence of God

You will make known to me the way of life; In Your presence is fullness of joy; In Your right hand there are pleasures forever.

Psalm 16:11 (NASB)

Father God,

I love this prayer time together where I can immerse myself in Your Presence. Living with You in Your Presence IS the path to life. I am so thankful that You are teaching me to live in this way because that is where all joy and peace begins. Oh, but there are so many distractions all day long that pull me away from You. Help me, help me, help me Lord, to intentionally talk to You, simply and plainly, all through the day. Remind me to give You praise because You are a perfect and good God. The more I practice being in Your Presence during my days, the more my life falls into place. I will be patient with myself as I am progressing in this new practice. I will be grateful for every step in Your direction. I am thanking You now for Your help and guidance. In Jesus' name I pray.

Song Suggestion: In Your Presence *by* Jeremy Camp

January 16

Trust God

But when I am afraid, I will put my trust in you. I praise God for what he has promised. I trust In God, so why should I be afraid? What can mere mortals do to me?

Psalm 56:3-4 (NLT)

Father God,

Thank You that I can trust in You. You are faithful. You are always with me. You have my back. I praise You and I thank You because I can put my faith and trust in You. I admit that I have untold fears, stressors, and anxieties in my life. Too many times my expectations are not met. Sometimes, I get mad at You when things do not go my way. But I am taking time this morning to focus on trusting You. I am slowing down, I am still, I am breathing You in and leaning on You. I am reminding myself that I can trust You with everything in my life. Thank You for being with me, thank you for carrying me, thank You for helping me even when I do not see. You are my good, good Father whom I trust and as a result I can live in Your perfect peace. I gratefully pray in Jesus' name today.

Song Suggestion: Trust in God *by* Elevation Worship

Forgiving

For if you forgive people their trespasses [their reckless and willful sins, leaving them, letting them go, and giving up resentment] your heavenly Father will also forgive you. But if you do not forgive others their trespasses [their reckless and willful sins, leaving them, letting them go, and giving up resentment], neither will your Father forgive you your trespasses.

Matthew 6:14-15 (Amp)

Father God,

As part of the "Our Father" prayer, I have said, "Forgive us our trespasses/debts as we forgive those who trespass against us" countless times. I confess today that I have routinely said it (without thoroughly comprehending) and I have not consistently done it. I have held grudges against family, friends, coworkers, and peers. I have held onto anger over things people have said or done to me. I have been unforgiving countless times. I realize how difficult forgiving others truly is. So, I ask You, Holy Spirit to help me to learn to forgive completely as Jesus has taught and modeled. Clear my vision so that I can see who I need to forgive. Give me the strength, wisdom, and determination to do so. I thank You for forgiving me and I receive Your help right now so that I can give

You glory and live the peaceful, forgiving way that You command. I ask for Your help in Jesus' name.

Song Suggestion: The Lord's Prayer (It's Yours) *by* Matt Maher

January 18

My Words

A man's [moral] self shall be filled with the fruit of his mouth; and with the consequence of his words he must be satisfied [whether good or evil]. Death and life are in the power of the tongue, and they who indulge in it shall eat the fruit of it [for death or life].

Proverbs 18:20-21 (Amp)

Father God,

This morning, I put my focus on my words - what I say to myself and others. Teach me so that I learn and truly understand that my words have consequences, and my words have power. Lord, this is a truth that I need to think about, to ponder, to internalize. Up to this point, I have just said whatever pops out of my mouth. But You are teaching me that I need to be more mindful, more intentional about what I say as death and life are in my power. I ask the Holy Spirit to begin working with me on helping me think about what I say each day. Starting today, I am going to try to focus on what I am saying to myself and to others and I will think about the consequences of my words. Help me to speak life! Father, Spirit, Jesus be with me, guide me, correct me, and help me on this journey. I pray this prayer in Jesus' holy name.

Song Suggestion: Speak Life *by* Toby Mac

Anxiety

Come to Me, all you who labor and are heavy-laden and overburdened, and I will cause you to rest. [I will ease and relieve and refresh your souls.] Take My yoke upon you and learn of Me, for I am gentle (meek) and humble (lowly) in heart, and you will find rest (relief and ease and refreshment and recreation and blessed quiet) for your souls. For My yoke is wholesome (useful, good - not harsh, hard, sharp, or pressing, but comfortable, gracious, and pleasant), and My burden is light and easy to be borne.

Matthew 11:28-30 (Amp)

Father God and Jesus,

This morning, I am coming to You with my worries, my anxieties, all my stresses, all my problems, my weariness, my past mistakes. I am sitting at Your feet, and I am laying these burdens down. I am letting them go and I am receiving Your rest. I am sitting quietly in Your rest, enjoying Your peaceful, tranquil, life altering Presence. I am joining my spirit with Yours. I am moving forward into this day with You at my side. And when the burdens come back into my mind, I am casting them away and focusing on Your rest. I will remember that You are with me, You are covering me with Your love. I am giving You thanks. I will give You thanks and praise all day long as I rest in You. I pray in Jesus' name.

Song Suggestion: Love is Here *by* Tenth Avenue North

January 20

Thankful

Oh that men would give thanks to the LORD for His goodness, And for His wonderful works to the children of men! Let them sacrifice the sacrifices of thanksgiving, and declare His works with rejoicing.

Psalm 107:21-22 (NKJV)

Father God,

I confess that You are so, so good to me! You have done so much for me. I give thanks and praise to You right now for all the loving kindness that You have surrounded me with. I give thanks for ALL You have done, are doing, and promised to do for me. I specifically thank you for the blessings in my life. (**Note:** *Communicate to God all the personal blessings you are thankful for.*) I am forever grateful to You, my Lord and my Father. With a grateful heart I pray in Jesus' name today.

Song Suggestion: Gratitude *by* Brandon Lake

January 21

Prayer

In those days when you pray, I will listen. If you look for me wholeheartedly, you will find me.

Jeremiah 29:12-13 (NLT)

Father God,

When I read this scripture, I am filled with relief that You are a God who listens. I am realizing more and more how much I need You. I cannot live my life well without You by my side. I am so grateful that I can call on You, I can come to You, and I can share my life in all its ups and downs with You in prayer. I am so, so grateful that You will hear and listen to me. Thank You for listening to me each time I pray. Thank You for being with me. I know that I can live my best life with You as I look to You to guide me and help me every day. Inspire me to be consistent in my willingness to spend time in communication, in prayer, every, single day. More than anything else, it is You I need in my life. I pray this in Jesus' name.

Song Suggestion: What a Friend We Have in Jesus *by* Alan Jackson

January 22

Seek God

Glory in His holy name; let the hearts of those rejoice who seek the Lord! Seek the Lord and His strength; yearn for and seek His face and to be in His presence continually!

1 Chronicles 16:10-11 (Amp)

Father God, Jesus and Holy Spirit,

Your name is holy. All glory and praise I offer to You this morning. I am seeking You and Your holy Presence this morning. I am quieting my mind and my soul and focusing only on You. This is my favorite time of day - when I can come to You and sit serenely in Your Presence. I seek all You are. I ask You to fill me with Your love, hope, joy and peace.

You are my strength, and You are all I need today and always, no matter what is going on around me. I pray in Jesus' name.

Song Suggestion: First Things First *by* Consumed by Fire

Discouragement

It is the Lord Who goes before you; He will [march] with you; He will not fail you or let you go or forsake you; [let there be no cowardice or flinching, but] fear not, neither become broken [in spirit - depressed, dismayed, and unnerved with alarm].

Deuteronomy 31:8 (Amp)

Father God,

I come before You this morning with a humble attitude. I admit that there are times that I feel fear, depression, disappointment, and an overall feeling that I am broken. I also admit that I, all too often, do not invite You into my life to help me with these emotions. Help me to truly understand that Your words of old can lift my spirits and can help me turn my thinking and feelings from reactionary to uplifting. From a downward spiral to an upward trajectory. Help me remember, always, no matter what the circumstances are or what I am feeling that You are with me! Yes, You are with me and You will never leave me, and I know, You will lead me to a better place. I do not need to wallow in my discouraging situation. I can lift my hand to You and thank You and praise You because You are putting Your hand in mine and pulling me into Your Presence. Thank You for being so faithful to me. Thank You for planting seeds of joy and hope deep within me. In Jesus' name I pray today.

Song Suggestion: I am Not Alone *by* Kari Jobe

January 24

God's Love

As far as the east is from the west so far has He removed our transgressions from us. As a father loves and pities his children, so the Lord loves and pities those who fear Him [with reverence, worship, and awe].

Psalm 103:12-13 (Amp)

Father God,

I want to start my day worshiping and praising You. You are my holy, sovereign Father. You love me and I am Your child. I am so thankful for Your love. I am so thankful that You not only forget about my sins, my mistakes, my flaws, but You remove them from me. Your Word says that You remove my sins as far as the east is from the west. Thank You for Your mercy. Thank You for Your forgiveness. I am in awe of that kind of love.

You are an amazing and loving Father and I choose to honor You in all I do today. I pray this prayer in Jesus' name.

Song Suggestion: East to West *by* Casting Crowns

Hope

[What, what would have become of me] had I not believed that I would see the Lord's goodness in the land of the living! Wait and hope for and expect the Lord; be brave and of good courage and let your heart be stout and enduring. Yes, wait for and hope for and expect the Lord.

Psalm 27:13-14 (Amp)

Father God,

Where would I be without You? I am so grateful that I have You in my life, steering me in ways that will bring life and life overflowing. I believe I will see and experience Your goodness in my life. I am waiting for You with expectation and excitement! Even when things are not going my way or I must do hard things, I choose to believe that You are working things out for my good. I choose to be brave and to have a good attitude. I choose to endure as I wait and hope for and expect Your goodness and grace. You are truly my hope for today, tomorrow, and forever. I am gratefully praying with faith filled expectations in Jesus' name today.

Song Suggestion: Goodness of God *by* Bethel Music and Jenn Johnson

January 26

Perseverance

Do not, therefore, fling away your fearless confidence, for it carries a great and glorious compensation of reward. For you have need of steadfast patience and endurance, so that you may perform and fully accomplish the will of God, and thus receive and carry away [and enjoy to the full] what is promised.

Hebrews 10:35-36 (Amp)

God, Our Father,

You know how hard it is to live a life that is faith-filled with behavior that illuminates that faith. While I do have some victories, I also have lots of failed moments when I forget that I have You as my rock, my strength, my healer, my provider. I forget that You are faithful. I often do whatever I want, especially in tough times. Help me, help me to persevere each day with You. Help me to endure all tough times, trusting that You are with me. Help me to let You guide me so that I can face each day doing Your will and not mine. Give me a spirit of endurance, of persistence and of perseverance. Thank You for consistently being my helper. In Jesus' name I pray.

Song Suggestion: Stand in Faith *by* Danny Gokey

I am a Child of God

But to as many as did receive and welcome Him, He gave the authority (power, privilege, right) to become the children of God, that is, to those who believe in (adhere to, trust in, and rely on) His name-

John 1:12 (Amp)

Father God,

I am so filled with gratitude at the thought that because I welcome Jesus into my life, I am Your child. I am a child of You, the most holy God! You have given me the most precious gift ever. Because of my faith, I get the privilege of trusting You as a small child trusts their dad. I am declaring my faith and trust in You this morning. I am remembering to trust You with all aspects of my life. You are my Father and I am loved, cherished, and cared for as Your child. Oh, how I give thanks and praise to You for this gift. Today, I will remember to live like I am loved! I pray in Your Son, Jesus' name.

Song Suggestion: I'm So Blessed *by* Cain

January 28

Motivation

Today I have given you the choice between life and death, between blessings and curses. Now I call on heaven and earth to witness the choice you make. Oh, that you would choose life, so that you and your descendants might live!

Deuteronomy 30:19 (NLT)

Father God,

You are life. All Your ways are good, pure, and true. You give me the choice every minute of each day to choose to do things Your way, the right way, leading to life or to choose to do things my own way. I am deciding right now that I will follow You to the best of my ability. I will rely on You to help me. I trust that You will be with me. I choose You, Father, Spirit, Jesus. I choose to live the life that You are offering me. With gratitude and praise, I pray in Jesus' name.

Song Suggestion: The Blessing *by* John Waller

Pray for Others

FIRST OF all, then, I admonish and urge that petitions, prayers, intercessions, and thanksgivings be offered on behalf of all men,

3 For such [praying] is good and right, and [it is] pleasing and acceptable to God our Savior, Who wishes all men to be saved and [increasingly] to perceive and recognize and discern and know precisely and correctly the [divine] Truth.

1 Timothy 2:1,3-4 (Amp)

Father God,

I am so thankful that You hear me whenever I pray. I thank You for the gift of other people in my life. I am especially thankful for... (**Note:** *Communicate to God the specific people in your life that you are thankful for*). This morning, I want to pray for others who do not know You in a personal way. I especially want to pray for (**Note:** *Communicate to God individuals by name*). I pray that You will soften their hearts so when they hear Your truth from any source, their hearts and minds will open to You. I also pray for our country, Father God, give our leaders wisdom and the courage to do Your will. Help me to do Your will each day, help me help others to see and feel Your love. In Jesus' saving name I pray.

Song Suggestion: My Prayer for You *by* Alisa Turner

January 30

I Am... A Friend of God

"No longer do I call you servants, for a servant does not know what his master is doing; but I have called you friends, for all things that I heard from My Father I have made known to you.

John 15:15 (NKJV)

Father God,

I sit quietly and think about the fact that Your holy Son, Jesus, has called me friend. While I do not feel that it could be true because I am unworthy by all accounts, I thank You God, knowing that my feelings are not the truth, but what You say is the truth. So, Jesus, I am truly, deeply thankful that You are ALL things to me: my Lord, my Savior, and my Friend. I reach my hand to You and let Your truth, Your love and Your friendship wash over me as I begin this day. Help me to remember this love and friendship all through my days. I am Your friend, and You are mine. I pray gratefully in Jesus' name.

Song Suggestion: I Am a Friend of God *by* Phillips, Craig and Dean

I Will...

Don't be selfish; don't try to impress others. Be humble, thinking of others as better than yourselves. Don't look out only for your own interests, but take an interest in others, too.

Philippians 2:3-4 (NLT)

Father God,

Thank You for teaching me Your ways. I have so much to learn so that I can live more like You. Today I am setting the intention that I will live unselfishly, thinking about others' needs before my own. I will start at home with my family. I ask the Holy Spirit to guide my thinking so that I am aware of when my thoughts are centered on ME and my selfish desires. Make me aware of others and their needs. This will be a long-term undertaking but with Your help, I will show my love for You by loving others and being more and more selfless rather than selfish. I know that Your way is good and right and will lead to more joy and peace in my own life. I praise You because You are a God of loving kindness and gentleness. I pray in Jesus' name today.

Song Suggestion: Won't You be My Love *by* Mercy Me

February 1

Holy, Sovereign God

Each of these living beings had six wings, and their wings were covered all over with eyes, inside and out. Day after day and night after night they keep on saying, "Holy, holy, holy is the Lord God, the Almighty - the one who always was, who is and who is still to come." Whenever the living beings give glory and honor and thanks to the one sitting on the throne (the one who lives forever and ever), the twenty-four elders fall down and worship the one sitting on the throne (the one who lives forever and ever). And they lay their crowns before the throne and say, "You are worthy, O Lord our God, to receive glory and honor and power. For you created all things, and they exist because you created what you pleased."

Revelation 4:8-11 (NLT)

Holy, holy Father God,

I do not even come close to understanding how holy You are, how perfect, and how pure. I recognize that You are so far above and beyond me. I take this time to think about You on Your throne, enveloped in light, warmth, love, holiness. I am in awe of You. You are my Father, my creator. Open my soul so I can know You more. I open my spirit, my mind and invite You in. I stay here in Your holy Presence and am filled with quiet, peaceful awe. As I move through this day, I will remember our time together and I will know that

Your Presence is with me. I will lean into Your Presence today, full of hope, gratitude, and love for You. In Jesus' name I pray.

Song Suggestion: Surrounded by Holy (Acoustic) *by* Bethel Music, Zahriya Zachary

Praise

I will bless the LORD at all times; His praise shall continually be in my mouth. My soul will make its boast in the LORD; The humble will hear it and rejoice. Exalt the LORD with me, and let's exalt His name together. I sought the LORD and He answered me, and rescued me from all my fears.

Psalm 34:1-4 (NASB)

Father God,

I come before You this day to praise You and bless You. I declare Your goodness and I lift up Your name. I thank You that You are a Father who not only hears me but answers me. As I seek You and listen for Your guidance, I am filled with faith. I thank You, bless You and praise You because I can fall spiritually into Your arms, and You hold me with loving kindness, mercy, and love. I sit quietly with You now as I give You praise, honor and glory. It is all I have to give. I pray this prayer in Jesus' name.

Song Suggestion: We Praise You *by* Matt Redman

February 3

Wisdom

For the L*ORD gives wisdom; From His mouth come knowledge and understanding;*

Proverbs 2:6 (NASB)

God, My Father,

Thank You for Your wisdom in my life. You have ALL knowledge and understanding of all things. I humbly come before You and ask You to give me understanding of Your ways. I am so thankful that You are working with me and working in my life. I believe that I am growing closer to You. I believe that I am becoming more like You, ever so slowly. I believe that I am in Your hands, and You are shining Your light on me right now. I embrace Your light and all Your ways. Continue to give me Your wisdom, vision and understanding. I ask this in Jesus' name today.

Song Suggestion: Show me Your Ways *by* Thrive Worship featuring Leeland

February 4

Forgiven

I am writing to you who are God's children because your sins have been forgiven through Jesus.

1 John 2:12 (NLT)

Father God, Jesus, and Holy Spirit,

Thank You, thank You for forgiving my sins and for all the joy and hope that Your forgiveness brings. I am eternally grateful. There is no way that I can pay You for all You have done for me. I can, however, purposefully live my life - giving honor to You in how I think, what I do and what I say. I am purposefully living in Your love, mercy, and forgiveness each day. Help me to remember this amazing gift daily. In Jesus' name I pray.

Song Suggestion: My Offering *by* 33 Miles

Open Ears

If any man has ears to hear, let him be listening and let him perceive and comprehend. And He said to them, be careful what you are hearing. The measure [of thought and study] you give [to the truth you hear] will be the measure [of virtue and knowledge] that comes back to you - and more [besides] will be given to you who hear.

Mark 4:23-24 (Amp)

Father God,

I come before You this morning asking You to open my ears, my mind, and my heart to You. I acknowledge that Your truth and Your ways are often so different from mine. Your scripture today helps me to realize that the more effort and time I put into learning of You, the more knowledge and understanding You will give me. I ask that You give me a teachable heart. Give me a desire to carve out time to learn of You. I need You more and more. I ask this in Jesus' name.

Song Suggestion: Sacred Pages *by* John Waller

Joy

Go your way, eat your bread with joy, and drink your wine with a cheerful heart [if you are righteous, wise and in the hands of God], for God has already accepted your works.

Ecclesiastes 9:7 (Amp)

Father God,

Thank You for the simple things in life. Thank You for blessing me. I am so grateful and joyful when I think of all You have provided for me. I love that You want me to enjoy Your gifts. You are a giving, loving Father who accepts me as I am. I rest in that fact and sit contented and joyful right now in Your Presence. I meditate on Your joy and all the gifts that give me joy. I receive Your joy in this moment. I breathe it in. Guide me, I pray, to carry Your joy and contentment with me as I go about my day. I thank You that You are a good, good Father. In Jesus' holy name I pray this morning.

Song Suggestion: Did You Feel the Mountains Tremble *by* Delirious

Love God, Love Others

Let all men know and perceive and recognize your unselfishness (your considerateness, your forbearing spirit). The Lord is near [He is coming soon].

Philippians 4:5 (Amp)

Father God,

I close my eyes and think about how good You are to me. You are gracious, giving, merciful, longsuffering and patient with me. I am not consistently any of those things especially to the people closest to me. I ask You to help me. Help me go out today with the intention of being kinder, more compassionate, more merciful, more tolerant and patient to all those around me. I know that as I remember and practice, along with Your help, I will become more like you little by little. I thank You that You are near. I thank you for Your love. I thank You so much for Your patience with me. I thank You for helping me love others like You. In Jesus' name I pray.

Song Suggestion: The Generous Mr. Lovewell *by* MercyMe

Names of God

Elohim

This name is only written in the Hebrew language. The name traditionally refers to God as The Creator and Judge. Elohim signifies God's creative power and His authority and sovereignty.

IN THE beginning God (prepared, formed, fashioned, and) created the heavens and the earth.

Genesis 1:1 (Amp)

Father God,

You are the creator of all things. You are awesome and amazing. Your creation is vast and incomprehensible. I take this quiet moment to meditate on Your creation. I spend this time worshiping You, my God, Elohim, my creator. You breathe life into me and all living things. I join all Your creation in praising You, for You are so far above us all. I think about some of the amazing places that I have seen (**Note:** *Feel free to think about, identify and tell God about your favorite places*). Thank You for these wonderful places and for the blessings that I have received in getting to see them. I am in awe of the works of Your hands. Help me to slow down and open my eyes to Your beautiful creation that is all around me as I go through this day. I am praying this prayer gratefully in Jesus' name.

Song Suggestion: So Will I (100 Billion X) *by* Hillsong United

Jesus

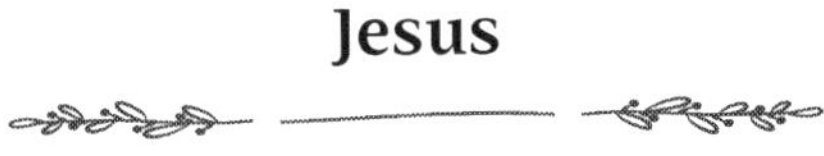

For at just the right time Christ will be revealed from heaven by the blessed and only almighty God, the King of all kings and Lord of all lords.

1 Timothy 6:15 (NLT)

Jesus,

This morning, I declare that You are the King of kings, and the Lord of lords as Your Father has spoken. You are blessed and worthy; You are our sovereign ruler. Thank You for coming to this earth, leaving Your kingdom with Your Father where You were worshiped continually. Thank You for trying to teach us Your ways even while many hated You and continually planned for Your harm. Yet, You rule now with love, joy, mercy, kindness, and compassion. You allow us to do what we please while trying to teach us the ways that will help us. I know that one day You will return where You will receive all the glory and praise that You are due. While I wait for that day, I will give You glory and praise every day. I will remember that You are my King and my Lord. I pray this in Jesus' holy name.

Song Suggestion: Here is Our King *by* David Crowder Band

February 10

Eternity Minded

It shall be said in that day, Behold our God upon Whom we have waited and hoped, that He might save us! This is the Lord, we have waited for Him; we will be glad and rejoice in His salvation.

Isaiah 25:9 (Amp)

Father God,

Help me to be eternity minded. Help me to live in such a way that I remember life's trials and troubles are temporary. Right now, I am rejoicing that You have saved me to live in perfect love and perfect peace with You forever. I can sing, praise, and honor You because I have such an awesome promise! You have given me the ultimate gift - the gift of life forever lived in Your kingdom with You, my loving Father. Although I do not know what eternity is exactly like, I do know that You will be there with Your perfect light. Your light will replace all darkness and there will be only joy. I will carry Your light and Your joy with me today. I pray that it will flow out to all those around me. In Jesus' name I pray.

Song Suggestion: I Can Only Imagine *by* MercyMe

February 11

Believing

Because if you acknowledge and confess with your lips that Jesus is Lord and in your heart believe (adhere to, trust in, and rely on the truth) that God raised Him from the dead, you will be saved.

Romans 10:9 (Amp)

Father God,

I confess right now that Jesus, Your one and only Son, is my Lord and my Savior. He is the Lord of my life, and I am striving to learn what that means as I journey on. I believe in my heart that Jesus was crucified on the cross for me, but He did not stay there. He rose from the dead. I believe that I am saved because I trust in Your truth. I am so grateful for Your plan to save me and bring me into Your family, into Your kingdom. I will forever praise You and thank You now and throughout all of time. Jesus, I believe in You, and I offer You all my gratitude and praise for all You have done. I owe all to You. I pray in Your good and holy name.

Song Suggestion: We Believe *by* Newsboys

Peace

And the effect of righteousness will be peace [internal and external], and the result of righteousness will be quietness and confident trust forever.

Isaiah 32:17 (Amp)

Father God,

You call me to live righteously, and Your promise is peace. I am so thankful that You are a God who sees me and understands me. You are loving and patient while leading me on the journey to perfect righteousness. Meanwhile I can rely on and trust in Jesus who has covered me in His righteousness. I lean into these promises, and I am filled with Your peace. As I raise my eyes to You, Your peace and goodness overwhelm me. I sit in stillness and am awed by the gift of Your peace. Help me to carry this peace close to my heart so others will see that Your peace is in me. And I will confidently trust in You and Your perfect ways of peace forever. In Jesus' name I pray today.

Song Suggestion: Tremble *by* Mosaic MSC

February 13

God's Will

And so, dear brothers and sisters, I plead with you to give your bodies to God because of all he has done for you. Let them be a living and holy sacrifice - the kind he will find acceptable. This is truly the way to worship him. Don't copy the behavior and customs of this world, but let God transform you into a new person by changing the way you think. Then you will learn to know God's will for you, which is good and pleasing and perfect.

Romans 12:1-2 (NLT)

Father God,

I worship You this morning. It is so easy to do in the quiet solitude of our time together. I pray that as I grow closer to You (spiritually), I will practice more acts of worship in my day-to-day life. I ask the Holy Spirit to renew my mind continually so that I will put you first in all areas of my life. Help me to see the difference in Your ways and my ways and the ways in the world in which I live. I want to learn, and I want to please You most of all because of all You have done for me. Thank You for Your patient guidance. Thank You that You have a plan and a purpose for me. Even though I don't always see Your will, I will walk step by step with expectant hope and joy knowing that You are by my side. I pray this in Jesus' name.

Song Suggestion: I Give You My Heart *by* Michael W. Smith

Thoughts/Mindset

For those who are according to the flesh and are controlled by its unholy desires set their minds on and pursue those things which gratify the flesh, but those who are according to the Spirit and are controlled by the desires of the Spirit set their minds on and seek those things which gratify the [Holy] Spirit. Now the mind of the flesh [which is sense and reason without the Holy Spirit] is death [death that comprises all the miseries arising from sin, both here and hereafter]. But the mind of the [Holy] Spirit is life and [soul] peace [both now and forever].

Romans 8:5-6 (Amp)

Father God, Holy Spirit, and Jesus,

I ask You to give me a new mindset! I praise You and thank You and am in awe at the mindset of You, Jesus, who had purpose and intentionality in all Your thoughts and actions. I often live my life thinking, "What do I want today?" rather than "What do You want for me today?" Help me change my thoughts and mindset so that I am becoming more like You. Your Word tells me that the mind of the Spirit is life and peace. You are amazing that You offer me these gifts. I thank You right now for Your constant attempts to mold my thoughts so that I can have life to the fullest along with peace forever more. Although I am not worthy, I put my hands up to grasp Yours and invite You to open my mind to Your Holy Spirit. I humbly and gratefully pray this prayer in Jesus' name today.

Song Suggestion: Echo (Live) *by* Elevation Worship feat Tauren Wells

February 15

The Presence of God

"If you love Me, keep My commandments. And I will pray the Father, and He will give you another Helper, that He may abide with you forever- the Spirit of truth, whom the world cannot receive, because it neither sees Him nor knows Him; but you know Him, for He dwells with you and will be in you. I will not leave you orphans; I will come to you.

John 14:15-18 (NKJV)

Father God,

How can I express my deepest gratitude for the gift of Your Holy Spirit? You have given me the ultimate helper who is always with me. I may not always feel Your Holy Spirit, but by faith, I know that He never leaves me. I ask the Holy Spirit now to awaken my heart, soul and mind to Your Presence and the reality that I can enter into Your Presence any time by leaning into You. I can live here in Your Presence all day long, not only when I am alone during this special prayer time that we share. I can ask You to help me with each task I do, and I can thank You while I am doing it. I can communicate throughout the day, sharing my weaknesses, asking You to come alongside me while acknowledging Your goodness and thanking You for blessings that come to mind. I thank You Father and Jesus for this gift to be with You through Your Holy Spirit for all my days. I pray in Jesus' name.

Song Suggestion: Breathe On Me *by* John Waller

February 16

Trust God

Even youths shall faint and be weary, and [selected] young men shall feebly stumble and fall exhausted; but those who wait for the Lord [who expect, look for, and hope in Him] shall change and renew their strength and power; they shall lift their wings and mount up [close to God] as eagles [mount up to the sun]; they shall run and not be weary, they shall walk and not faint or become tired.

Isaiah 40:30-31 (Amp)

Father God,

As I grow closer and closer to You, I am putting my hope in You more and more. You are the One who gives me strength each day. You are the One who gives me purpose. You are the One who gives me energy and wisdom to do what I need to do. Where would I be without You? I need You. I am so blessed that I can lean on You, I can depend on You, I can trust in You. The closer I lean, the more You help. When I grow weary from the challenges I face, I will wait for You. I am putting all my hope in You. While I am hoping and waiting, I will praise You for giving me strength and power. You will help me run and not be weary. You will help me continue to walk and not faint. I pray with gratitude that I can trust in and rely on You. In Jesus' name I pray.

Song Suggestion: Silence *by* JWLKRS Worship

Forgiving

And even if he sins against you seven times in a day, and turns to you seven times and says, I repent [I am sorry], you must forgive him (give up resentment and consider the offense as recalled and annulled).

Luke 17:4 (Amp)

Father God,

Can I really forgive someone who hurts me, betrays me, who disappoints me, who is rude to me, who consistently is unkind and does unkind things to me? You say that I can. You say that I must, and I must do it over and over again. Oh, that is a really challenging task. But I will choose to obey Jesus' command. I will choose forgiveness even if my feelings are not there yet. I believe my feelings will catch up eventually. I ask You to help me forgive. Fill Me with Your love and Your peace so that these are the feelings that will drive my behaviors, my thoughts, my attitudes. Holy Spirit, I believe that You can help me forgive and I am asking You to help me let go of all bitterness, resentment, and anger so that I can live the life of joy, hope and peace that You want for me. Thank You for Your forgiveness, grace, and mercy that You have shown me. I pray with gratitude in Jesus' name today.

Song Suggestion: What If *by* Matthew West

February 18

My Words

The Lord GOD has given Me the tongue of disciples, so that I may know how to sustain the weary one with a word. He awakens Me morning by morning, He awakens My ear to listen as a disciple.

Isaiah 50:4 (NASB)

Father God,

Thank You for allowing me to be one of Your disciples. I am so grateful for all You are teaching me. You teach me truth and wisdom. I love this scripture because I believe that You are the One who awakens me. I invite and welcome You to awaken me every morning, to awaken my ears to listen to You. Especially guiding me to use my words to do Your works - to lift others up, to give encouragement, to sustain the weary. Let Your wisdom come out of my mouth. I submit my mouth to You right now. I use my words to start my day glorifying You and thanking You. I use my words to speak some of Your promises over my life and over the ones I love: You will never leave me. You will give me strength to do all things through Jesus. You hold me up with Your right hand. You are my Shepherd and I have all that I need. I can cast my cares on You. You have given me Your peace. Thank You that I can speak Your words of life. I pray with deep gratitude and praise in Jesus' name.

Song Suggestion: Words *by* Hawk Nelson

February 19

Anxiety

Do Not fret or have any anxiety about anything, but in every circumstance and in everything, by prayer and petition (definite requests), with thanksgiving, continue to make your wants known to God. And God's peace [shall be yours, that tranquil state of a soul assured of its salvation through Christ, and so fearing nothing from God and being content with its earthly lot of whatever sort that is, that peace] which transcends all understanding shall garrison and mount guard over your hearts and minds in Christ Jesus.

Philippians 4:6-7 (Amp)

Father God,

I am grateful for so many things. (**Note:** *Communicate to God what You are grateful for.*) I also have worries about many things. (**Note:** *Communicate what is worrying you.*) I am thanking You because You hear me today. I am thanking You because You are working even If I don't see any change right away. I am accepting Your will for me to be content even if my circumstances are not perfect and even when problems arise. I am putting my faith in You. Thank You for listening. Thank You for caring about me and all my circumstances. Thank You for helping me overcome all my worries. Thank You for Your peace which is guarding my heart and mind. I am focusing on Your peace and faithfulness right now as I sit quietly in Your calming, tranquil Presence. You are truly a loving Father. I give You my anxieties today and I let them go as I pray in Jesus' name.

Song Suggestion: Fall on Me *by* NEEDTOBREATHE feat Carly Pearce

February 20

Thankful

For sin is the sting that results in death, and the law gives sin its power. But thank God! He gives us victory over sin and death through our Lord Jesus Christ.

1 Corinthians 15:56-57 (NLT)

Father God,

I am so thankful for the blessing of salvation. I am thankful for the victory over sin and death that Jesus has given me. I am thankful that I can live with You forever. My spirit has been permanently united with and grafted in Your Spirit. I can live under the banner of Your love, Your protection, Your provision. You are taking care of me now and forever. I am filled with hope in You and gratitude to You. This morning, I lift my heart, mind and soul and say thanks be to God! Thank You Jesus, for all You have done for me and given to me. I choose to live knowing (profoundly understanding deep in my soul) that I have victory over sin and over death. I choose to live with joy and gratitude for this victory. This prayer of thanksgiving is said in my Lord, Jesus' name today.

Song Suggestion: Thank You Jesus for the Blood (Live) *by* Charity Gayle

Prayer

I have called upon You, for You will hear me, O God; Incline Your ear to me, and hear my speech.

Psalm 17:6 (NKJV)

God, my Father,

Thank You for hearing all my prayers. I bring all my thoughts, my questions, my worries, my problems, even my doubts and I can talk to You about them. I can bring all my joys and celebrations to You too! (**Note**: *Communicate to God whatever is on your mind today.*) Thank You for listening, for guiding me and for answering me. Help me to be open to hear from You. I sit quietly in Your Presence with an expectant heart and mind. I praise You while I wait to hear from You. I praise You and thank You because You are my Father in heaven Who listens. In Jesus' name I pray today.

Song Suggestion: Same God *by* Elevation Worship

February 22

Seek God

"So I say to you, ask, and it will be given to you; seek, and you will find; knock, and it will be opened to you. For everyone who asks receives, and the one who seeks finds, and to the one who knocks, it will be opened.

Luke 11:9-10 (NASB)

Father God,

Here I am in Your Presence again, at the beginning of the day that You have given me. I am here to seek Your holy Presence and to sit quietly with You. I believe that You are here with me. I believe that as I keep asking, I will receive. I believe that if I keep knocking, You open doors for me. I am knocking and I am asking for… (**Note**: *Communicate with God about any requests that you have*). I am so thankful that You are the living God who can be found. I am so thankful that You are working in my life, even when I cannot see it. I thank You and praise You always. In Jesus' name I pray.

Song Suggestion: Hosanna (Praise is Rising) *by* Paul Baloche

February 23

Discouragement

Now David was greatly distressed, for the people spoke of stoning him, because the soul of all the people was grieved, every man for his sons and his daughters. But David strengthened himself in the Lord his God.

1 Samuel 30:6 (NKJV)

Father God,

I come to You this morning admitting that I can be (or I am) very discouraged, despondent, disappointed in the way things are going in my life (or in a specific area in my life). I know that You are good and that You are with me, but I confess that I don't always feel that way. I am thankful for this scripture because I can see that David had very real reasons to be utterly despondent and in complete despair. But David chose to turn away from these feelings and he was strengthened and encouraged in You. Lord, I pray that You will help me have such faith and trust in You as David did. I ask that You open my spirit and my mind to Your encouragement so that I can live the peaceful, joyful life that You have for me, even in the midst of my circumstances and troubles. I am overcoming because I am leaning, depending on, and trusting in You. I take a deep breath of renewal and encouragement as I pray these prayers in Jesus' name.

Song Suggestion: You Will Be Found *by* Natalie Grant feat. Cory Asbury

February 24

God's Love

The L*ORD your God in your midst, The Mighty One, will save; He will rejoice over you with gladness, He will quiet you with His love, he will rejoice over you with singing."*

Zephaniah 3:17 (NKJV)

God, my Father,

Sometimes I think that You are a God keeping track of all my faults, shortcomings, and sins. I wonder if You are mad at me. Because of Your Word, I can take comfort in the fact that You are with me! Thank You for being in my midst. You know me and all my faults and weaknesses and yet You love me and rejoice over me! I humbly accept Your love and tranquility and invite Your love into every part of my mind, heart, and soul. I let Your love fill me and I am sending my love right back to You. I love You, Lord, because You are the mighty One Who saves. I thank You and praise You for saving me and for the love You pour over me every day - even when I don't feel it. I pray with a heart full of love, gratitude, and praise in Jesus' name.

Song Suggestion: That's Enough *by* Brandon Heath

Hope

Through the LORD'S mercies we are not consumed, because His compassions fail not. They are new every morning; great is Your faithfulness. "The LORD is my portion," says my soul, "Therefore I hope in Him!"

Lamentations 3:22-24 (NKJV)

Father God,

You are a stable and faithful Father. You are my portion - You provide and care for me. I have lots of troubles and concerns right now, lots of things that I can complain about, be negative and focus on, but today I am choosing to think about Your care for me. I choose to think about Your faithful goodness, kindness, and compassion. I choose to turn my thoughts away from problems and negativity and focus on hoping in You, waiting expectantly for You. My soul reaches out to You, and I believe that You are holding my hand and infusing into me what I need. I sit quietly right now and let Your Presence saturate all of me. Thank You for being my living hope. I pray in Jesus' name today.

Song Suggestion: Great Is Thy Faithfulness *by* Carrie Underwood feat CeCe Wynans

February 26

Perseverance

So let's not get tired of doing what is good. At just the right time we will reap a harvest of blessing if we don't give up.

Galatians 6:9 (NLT)

Father God,

Thank You for allowing me to partner with You in this life. Thank You for giving me good works to do while I am here on earth. While I am thankful, there are times, if I am honest, when I am tired and weary of giving, giving, giving. I want to scream, "What about me?" But here in Your Word, You remind me to keep on going, keep on living for You, keep on shining light into this dark world. You remind me not to give up, not to give in! I believe that You are refreshing me. You pick me up, set me on my feet and help me to lean on You so I can continue to do Your will. Thank You for helping me when I am discouraged and weary. Thank You for giving me rest and giving me what I need to start over again. I take a minute this morning to slow down and inhale deeply. Thank You for helping me persevere so I can love and help others. I am determined to live for You each day. In Jesus' name I pray today.

Song Suggestion: Fear No More *by* Building 429

February 27

I am a Child of God

For He foreordained us (destined us, planned in love for us) to be adopted (revealed) as His own children through Jesus Christ, in accordance with the purpose of His will [because it pleased Him and was His kind intent]-

Ephesians 1:5 (Amp)

Father God,

I praise You this morning. I give You thanks. Deep, deep praise and heartfelt gratitude for the love You have shown me. You are the master planner - You made a way for me. I have been adopted by You and I am now Your child. I run into Your arms (spiritually) like a child running into a loving Father's arms. I am filled with gratitude, peace, love, joy, and eternal hope. I will be Your child forever. Just as a child is adopted and given a new life with all the benefits of a loving family, You have adopted me and given me a new life. I choose to immerse my mind and heart into Your love so that I can live like I am cherished and loved. I pray in Jesus' name today.

Song Suggestion: Who You Say I am *by* Hillsong Worship

Motivation

Therefore, my beloved brethren, be firm (steadfast), immovable, always abounding in the work of the Lord [always being superior, excelling, doing more than enough in the service of the Lord], knowing and being continually aware that your labor in the Lord is not futile [it is never wasted or to no purpose].

1 Corinthians 15:58 (Amp)

Father God,

I am setting my mind on You this morning. Let everything I do today be for You. Let my work, my chores, my daily tasks, my interactions with others, all be done for You. Let my motivation change from going through the motions of life to doing my best for others and ultimately for You. Let my motives be pure. Help me remember that all I do is important when I am serving You. Help me remain steadfast each day. Help me to remain focused on You all day long. I pray this prayer with a grateful heart in Jesus' name.

Song Suggestion: We Do Not Labor in Vain (Live) *by* Faithful

Pray for Others

You have not chosen Me, but I have chosen you and I have appointed you [I have planted you], that you might go and bear fruit and keep on bearing, and that your fruit may be lasting [that it may remain, abide], so that whatever you ask the Father in My Name [as presenting all that I AM], He may give it to you. This is what I command you: that you love one another.

John 15:16-17 (Amp)

Father God,

This morning, I sit quietly and think about what it means when You talk about choosing and bearing fruit. I do not feel worthy or qualified to be chosen and I do not consistently think of myself as "bearing fruit". However, I ask You to help me as I go out into the world. I would like to be a person who represents You well. Right now, while I am alone with You, I would like to pray for the people in my life who don't know about Your deep love or Your compassion, mercy, and salvation. I take time now to pray for… (**Note**: *Pray for people by name*). I pray that You will open their eyes, ears, hearts, and minds to You. Let them experience Your light, love, and forgiveness. I place them in Your hands today and I am grateful that You are working in all our lives. I pray that together, we would be Your light in this world. I pray in Jesus, our Savior's name.

Song Suggestion: These Days *by* Jeremy Camp

March 1

Holy, Sovereign God

The Lord *reigns, the peoples tremble! He sits enthroned above the cherubim, the earth quakes! The* Lord *is great in Zion, and He is exalted above all the peoples. May they praise Your great and awesome name; Holy is He.*

Psalm 99:1-3 (NASB)

Father God,

My faith is dependent on my knowledge and experience of You. Help me truly comprehend just how great, awesome, and holy You are. Open my eyes to that truth. In the world we live in, truth is hard to find. But You are the one true God, this I do believe. I praise You. I thank You for Your truth. You are my living God who will teach me as I open my heart and mind to You. I submit my life to You knowing that as my knowledge and experience of You is increasing, You are bringing me life, light, peace and all good things. I focus today on how great, how awesome, how holy you are! I pray in Jesus' name today.

Song Suggestion: Holy Forever *by* Chris Tomlin

March 2

Praise

For it is written: "AS I LIVE, SAYS THE LORD, TO ME EVERY KNEE WILL BOW, AND EVERY TONGUE WILL GIVE PRAISE TO GOD."

Romans 14:11 (NASB)

Father God,

Since the beginning of time, You have created us in Your image. You have created us to live with You and for You. You have said that one day everyone (believers of You and non-believers) will bow to You and give You praise. I am not waiting until "someday." I am intentionally bowing down before You right now in this holy and quiet moment. I am declaring that You are my holy and almighty Father. You are the only Lord of all. You are mighty and deserve all praise, honor, and glory. I am praising You now and will praise You forever. I am thankful that I have this time to continue to grow closer to You as I put You first in my life every day. I pray in Jesus' name today.

Song Suggestion: Father, Spirit, Jesus *by* Casting Crowns

March 3

Wisdom

Look carefully then how you walk! Live purposefully and worthily and accurately, not as the unwise and witless, but as wise (sensible, intelligent people), making the very most of the time [buying up each opportunity], because the days are evil.

Ephesians 5:15-16 (Amp)

Father God,

I want to please You. I want to walk in Your ways and honor You. I want to live with one purpose and that is to live for You. Today's scripture tells me to walk as the wise. The truth is that I need Your help to do this! So many unwise choices tempt me in this world. Please help me to hear You. Put Your truth in my heart, soul, and mind. Guide me to read Your Word and enable me to understand it and apply it. I am thanking You now for all You are doing to help me grow in wisdom and truth. I pray in Jesus' name today.

Song Suggestion: My Desire *by* Jeremy Camp

March 4

Forgiven

I, even I, am He Who blots out and cancels your transgressions, for My own sake, and I will not remember your sins.

Isaiah 43:25 (Amp)

Father God,

You are so good and kind that You would choose to forget all my mistakes, all the times I did what I wanted - not what You wanted. You have forgotten all the unkind and selfish things that I have thought, said, and done. You have canceled all my sins. I have let You down so, so many times. I have lived my life ignoring You or forgetting about You. I am sorry for all my sins. I am sorry that I have let You down. I am so grateful for Your forgiveness. I praise You that I can let go of all my guilt because You have not condemned me. No, You continue to give me more chances to get it right. I take time this morning to meditate on the deep gratitude I have for You, Father, for all Your love and mercy. I send my gratitude and love to You for the joy and peace that come from belonging to such a merciful and loving Father. I pray this prayer in Jesus,' my Savior's name.

Song Suggestion: Son of Suffering *by* Bethel Music, David Funk

March 5

Open Ears

He who has ears [to hear], let him be listening and let him consider and perceive and comprehend by hearing.

Matthew 13:9 (Amp)

Father God,

Jesus repeats Himself in the gospels to tell us that He wants us to not only hear His words but also heed them. I come to You now asking You to open my ears. Help me to not only read and/or hear Your words, but help me to understand, remember and then apply Your principles into my thoughts and actions. Open doors of opportunity for me to encounter Your Word. Ignite a yearning in me to seek You, hear You and obey You. Holy Spirit, I ask You to hear this prayer this morning and help me. I pray these things in Jesus' name.

Song Suggestion: I'm Listening *by* Chris McLarney

Joy

My lips will shout for joy when I sing praises to You; and my soul, which You have redeemed.

Psalm 71:23 (NASB)

Father God,

Thank You that You have made a way for me. Thank You that You have given me a clear direction to help me to live a more joy filled life. Help me to remember to praise You, thank You, and remember how You have redeemed me and saved me. I am free to live an abundant life focused on You and filled with Your joy and peace. Help me to let these truths sink into the deepest parts of my mind and heart so that I can live each day with You and for You, wrapped in Your peace and joy. I WILL shout for joy and sing Your praises today, Lord. In Jesus' name I pray.

Song Suggestion: Shout for Joy *by* Paul Baloche

Love God, Love Others

You shall not take revenge or bear any grudge against the sons of your people, but you shall love your neighbor as yourself. I am the Lord.

Leviticus 19:18 (Amp)

Father God,

You are the holy, most high Lord, who knows what is BEST for me. You want Your children to love You and to love others and have communicated how to do this over and over. I do love You and am making gains in loving others. I need Your help in loving all those around me as You would like. I am asking for Your help to love others by forgiving and dropping all grudges against those who have hurt me. Help me to see who I need to forgive right now. Help me see who I am holding a grudge against. Help me to see who I can show God's love to. Right now, I put my will and my emotions in Your hands as I trust You to help me forgive and let go of resentment. I thank You that You are taking care of me. I thank You and praise You for Your direction, even as it is difficult. I know that obeying You and Your commands will lead to a more peaceful life and will lead me to live closer to You. I pray in Jesus' name today.

Song Suggestion: With Every Act of Love *by* Jason Gray

Names of God

Adonai

A divine Hebrew name translated as 'Lord' or 'Master' which signifies sovereignty over us.

"When I passed by you again and looked upon you, indeed your time was the time of love; so I spread My wing over you and covered your nakedness. Yes, I swore an oath to you and entered into a covenant with you, and you became Mine," says the Lord GOD.

Ezekiel 16:8 (NKJV)

Father God,

This morning, I fill my mind and heart with how holy and sovereign You are. You are my one and only Lord. I acknowledge that You are my Master whose commands are always for my good. You are here with me, protecting me, covering me, providing for me. I invite You to come to save me from myself and from the influences of the world around me. I give You all my gratitude for allowing me to become Yours. I think about all Your promises that You have given. Promises to never leave me, promises to meet all my needs, promises to rejoice over me, promises to comfort and guide me as I seek You, promises to give me peace, joy, hope as I obey and trust in You. And so, I praise You with all that is within me, Adonai, my Lord forever. In Jesus' name I pray.

Song Suggestion: Love To Say Your Name *by* John Waller

March 9

Jesus

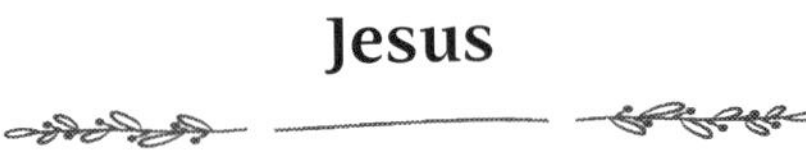

Thomas said to Him, "Lord, we do not know where You are going, and how can we know the way?" Jesus said to him, "I am the way, the truth, and the life. No one comes to the Father except through Me.

John 14:5-6 (NKJV)

Jesus,

As I live my life, I often get distracted, confused, stressed out. Remind me to come back to You. You are the "center". You said that You are the way, the truth, and the life. Teach me and show me what that means. I believe that as I purposely focus more and more on You, You will help me live in a more peaceful, joyful way. So, I start my day today with a resolve to follow You. To follow Your way and your truth as best as I know how. I believe that when I do this, You will lead me to life. A life of abundance and spiritual blessings. I pray to You, Jesus, this morning.

Song Suggestion: The Way (New Horizon) *by* Pat Barrett

March 10

Eternity Minded

This letter is from Paul, a slave of God and an apostle of Jesus Christ. I have been sent to proclaim faith to those God has chosen and to teach them to know the truth that shows them how to live godly lives. This truth gives them confidence that they have eternal life, which God-who does not lie-promised them before the world began.

Titus 1:1-2 (NLT)

Father God,

You have promised us, Your believers and followers, a guarantee from of old - the guarantee of eternal life. I don't like to think about death but if I focus on all I am gaining for eternity, I can rejoice that I have faith and am filled with hope. You will wipe away all pain, all sorrow, all anxiety. I will be in Your Presence! I will actually be with You, basking in Your light, Your warmth, Your peace. No one can take me away from You or Your kingdom. This hope and faith give me joyful anticipation. It motivates me to continue to live with You now and to share Your love with all. Thank You for Your promises that I carry with me in my heart. I am sitting quietly right now and imagining Your light, Your warmth, and Your peace streaming all around me as I start this day. I pray with gratitude in Jesus' name.

Song Suggestion: Hymn of Heaven *by* Phil Wickham

March 11

Believing

And just as Moses lifted up the serpent in the desert [on a pole], so must [so it is necessary that] the Son of Man be lifted up [on the cross], in order that everyone who believes in Him [who cleaves to Him, trusts Him, and relies on Him] may not perish, but have eternal life and [actually] live forever!

John 3:14-15 (Amp)

Jesus,

I am humbled and in awe as I (spiritually) sit at Your feet. I read how You knew that death on the cross was coming. You knew of the horror that was on the way, yet You put Your own will aside. By doing such an amazing act of love and obedience to the Father, You have saved me. I believe in You. I believe that it is Your righteousness, Your holiness that fills me. No matter how "good" I am, I will never be good enough to be thought of as righteous or holy. I close my eyes and think about being with You, surrounded by Your love now and forever. I can only raise my hands, my voice, my songs, my heart, and my life to You for all You have done for me. May my belief, praise, and gratitude please You today. I pray in Your holy, saving name.

Song Suggestion: What He's Done *by* Passion feat Kristian Stanfill, Tasha Cobbs Leonard, Anna Golden

March 12

Peace

THEREFORE, SINCE we are justified (acquitted, declared righteous, and given a right standing with God) through faith, let us [grasp the fact that we] have [the peace of reconciliation to hold and to enjoy] peace with God through our Lord Jesus Christ (the Messiah, the Anointed One).

Romans 5:1 (Amp)

Father God,

I put my faith in You. I believe that You have made a way for me to be able to come before You, as sinful as I am, knowing that You are a holy, perfect God. Because of my faith in You and in Jesus, You have forgiven me and You accept me as I am. Even though I do not deserve it, I have peace with You. Help me to remember that, as I often do not feel this peace. Empower me to purposefully tap into Your peace that lives inside me. Help me to live in peace with all those around me. The more that I intentionally set my mind to live in Your peace, the more peace I will have. Thank You for Your peace.

Thank You for giving me faith and the wisdom to continue to pursue You and Your peaceful ways. I sit quietly for a few minutes this morning to let Your peace fill me before I start this day. I pray in Jesus' name.

Song Suggestion: Peace of Christ *by* Tommy Walker

March 13

God's Will

Lean on, trust in, and be confident in the Lord with all your heart and mind and do not rely on your own insight or understanding. In all your ways know, recognize, and acknowledge Him, and He will direct and make straight and plain your paths.

Proverbs 3:5-6 (Amp)

Father God,

You are faultless. You are omniscient. Your ways are perfect, and Your truth is perfect. There are times when I do not understand Your ways, but I know that Your ways are so far above me. You see the entire picture and I cannot. So, I am humbling myself again before You. I am deciding that I will do my best to do Your will, to follow You. I will lean on and trust You even if I do not understand. I am so thankful that You will look out for me, You will make a way for me. You are helping me even though I may not see it.

Thank You that You are a God whom I can trust. Help me to recognize when You are at work in my life. Help me to remember to acknowledge You for Your amazing plans. Help me to be open to You as You direct me, as You show me Your perfect will and as You make my paths straight. The more I accept Your help and do things Your way, the easier my life will be. Oh, how I need You. I ask all these things in Jesus' name.

Song Suggestion: Your Way *by* KB and Britt Nicole

March 14

Thoughts/Mindset

Make me understand the way of Your precepts; so shall I meditate on and talk of Your wondrous works.

Psalm 119:27 (Amp)

Father God,

You have given me a gift which can change my life and bring me closer to You. The gift of a mindset based on You and Your life-giving ways. Thank You that when I am angry, I can meditate on forgiveness and mercy while remembering all the mercy You have poured on me. Thank You that when I am worrying and/or feeling stress and anxiety over the circumstances in my life, I can meditate on the peace that Jesus has given to me, and I can place my trust in You and remember all the times that You have helped me and provided for me. Thank You that when I am hurt or disappointed, I can meditate on how much You love me and what Jesus did to show such deep and eternal love for me. Holy Spirit, I ask that You give me thoughts of all You are and all Your wonderful ways. I am so grateful that You are faithful. I praise You and thank You that as I meditate on You, You straighten me out and help me with whatever I face. Oh, how good You are. I gratefully pray in Jesus' holy name.

Song Suggestion: Beautiful Life *by* Pat Barrett

The Presence of God

The Lord has taken away His judgments against you, He has cleared away your enemies. The King of Israel, the Lord, is in your midst; You will no longer fear disaster.

Zephaniah 3:15 (NASB)

Father God,

Thank You for being in my midst. I ask that You help increase my awareness of You and help me to be in Your Presence as I go about my day. Help me to intentionally do ALL my tasks for You. Help me to be mindful that I am in Your Presence, and I am working for You, not to please other people or get recognition but to do it all to demonstrate my love for You. I am so very blessed because I can talk to You all day long. I can lean on You. I can ask You for help. Lord, I want to please You more than anything else as You have shown me such mercy and grace. As I sit with You this morning, I thank You for guiding me and leading me into Your Presence. I look forward to living more and more in Your Presence as my life journey with You continues. I give You honor and praise for being such a loving and patient Father. In Jesus' name I pray this prayer.

Song Suggestion: Cover the Earth *by* Cody Carnes and Kari Jobe

March 16

Trust God

In God is my salvation and my glory; the rock of my strength, and my refuge, is in God. Trust in Him at all times, you people; pour out your heart before Him; God is a refuge for us. Selah.

Psalm 62:7-8 (NKJV)

*(Selah can mean to pause and calmly think about. The word, Selah, is found in several Old Testament books.)

Father God,

I come to You this morning, grateful that You are always here for me. Your Word tells me that You are my rock, my strength, my refuge. However, I am admitting now that I often forget these facts and go off on my own. I try to fix everything myself and then I worry, allowing my anxieties to take over my thoughts instead of putting my trust in You.

Remind me and help me, Holy Spirit to trust confidently in You. Help me to pour my heart out to You - I can share every single thing that is on my mind. You want to hear it all from me. I believe that You are listening and that You will show up in my life. I am pouring my heart out to You today Lord... (**Note**: *Communicate your specific, personal thoughts*). I trust You today. Thank You for being my salvation. Thank You for being my rock and my strength.

Thank You for being my refuge. I can never thank You enough. I pray in Jesus' trustworthy name.

Song Suggestion: I Trust Jesus *by* Matthew West, Jenn Johnson

March 17

Forgiving

Clothe yourselves therefore, as God's own chosen ones (His own picked representatives), [who are] purified and holy and well-beloved [by God Himself, by putting on behavior marked by] tenderhearted pity and mercy, kind feeling, a lowly opinion of yourselves, gentle ways, [and] patience [which is tireless and long-suffering, and has the power to endure whatever comes, with good temper]. Be gentle and forbearing with one another and, if one has a difference (a grievance or complaint) against another, readily pardoning each other; even as the Lord has [freely] forgiven you, so must you also [forgive].

Colossians 3:12-13 (Amp)

Father God,

Thank You for choosing me to be in Your family, to be a part of Your chosen people. You make me holy. I am well-beloved. I am grateful and overflowing with love for You as I do not deserve such kindness and tenderness. I will purposely seek to be compassionate, gracious, gentle, and patient with everyone around me. I believe that You give me power and strength to behave this way. I will choose to forgive others quickly and willingly. I will remember that You have forgiven me, and You continue to forgive me. Fill me with Your power - the power of love over all things. The power of mercy, compassion, and forgiveness. I ask for Your help with all these things in the One who modeled all these behaviors for me. I ask in Jesus' name.

Song Suggestion: Lay Me Down *by* Chris Tomlin

Our Words

But I tell you, on the day of judgment men will have to give account for every idle (inoperative, nonworking) word they speak. For by your words you will be justified and acquitted, and by your words you will be condemned and sentenced.

Matthew 12:36-37 (Amp)

Father God,

Your scripture this morning is extremely clear in teaching the importance of my words and that there are consequences for what I say. The consequences are eternal. While this is hard to hear, I know that I will need to meditate on and take this to heart. I hope to continue to be purposeful in what I say. I want to rid myself of careless, useless talk and use my words to help myself and others, words that will convey Your truth and Your love. Help me to use words that are full of mercy, compassion, kindness, love, peace, and hope. I cannot do this on my own. I am leaning on You Holy Spirit. I am asking You to help me say "right" things and help me avoid saying condemning, useless, unkind things. Oh, I need Your help. This morning, I start my day speaking life! I praise the Father, Son, and Holy Spirit. I thank You for teaching me and helping me. You have created me in Your image, and I am intentionally using my words to show You my gratitude! In Jesus' name I pray today.

Song Suggestion: Speak (Words Bring Life) *by* Trent & Siobhan

March 19

Anxiety

"These things I have spoken to you, that in Me you may have peace. In the world you will have tribulation; but be of good cheer, I have overcome the world."

John 16:33 (NKJV)

Father God,

You make me brave. You make me strong and courageous. You give me perfect peace. You have already warned me that I will suffer in this world. You have been clear that I will not get my own way just because I follow You. In fact, I may have more troubles. But I have faith that I am Your child! You have given me Jesus as my Savior. You have given me the Holy Spirit to guide me and comfort me. I have all I need in You. As anxiety and troubles arise, I will remember that You are my strength, You are my hope, You are my peace. You are holding me in Your arms. I will remember that You help me overcome all my distresses. In this moment, I breathe deeply and slowly while I give thanks and choose joy and peace (even if I don't feel these feelings yet). Thank You for being my overcomer and my refuge. I pray in gratitude in Jesus' name.

Song Suggestion: Be Alright *by* Evan Craft, Redimi2, Danny Gokey

March 20

Thankful

I will give thanks to the LORD with all my heart; I will tell of all Your wonders. I will rejoice and be jubilant in You; I will sing praise to Your name, O Most High.

Psalm 9:1-2 (NASB)

Father God,

I will praise You with my whole heart for all the marvelous things You have done! Your earth is full of miraculous and beautiful things - flowers, animals, waterfalls, mountains, forests, oceans, sunshine. You have given me wonderful things - family, friends, a home, a Savior, a future. I am thankful for all these blessings and so much more! I am deciding today that I will focus on Your blessings, and I am rejoicing in You. In this moment, I am breathing in and filling myself with joy because of You. I am praising and thanking You now and all throughout my day. You are an amazing, living, loving God. And forever You will be. I pray with profound gratitude in Jesus' name.

Song Suggestion: Thank You Lord *by* Chris Tomlin feat. Thomas Rhett and Florida Georgia Line

Prayer

I always thank my God when I pray for you Philemon, because I keep hearing about your faith in the Lord Jesus and your love for all of God's people. And I am praying that you will put into action the generosity that comes from your faith as you understand and experience all the good things we have in Christ.

Philemon 1:4-6 (NLT)

Father God,

I am praying that I would be like the apostle Paul who was consistently and continually praying. He was always praying for others. I am also praying that I would be like Philemon. I pray that I would have a strong faith in the Lord Jesus and that I would have a consistent love for all of God's people. I pray that I will put into action the generosity that comes from faith. I pray for all of us believers: I pray that we will truly understand and experience all the good things that we have in Christ. I pray that we will profoundly understand who You are and what You have done for us. I pray that we will experience You in a real and personal way and that our eyes will be opened more fully to Your love, more fully to Your light that is shining upon us so that we would shine in the dark world around us. I pray for blessings for us all as we turn our face toward heaven. I pray that we will worship You together. I worship You now in Jesus' name today.

Song Suggestion: Our Prayer *by* Rend Collective

Seek God

Glory in His holy name; let the hearts of those rejoice who seek and require the Lord [as their indispensable necessity]. Seek, inquire of and for the Lord, and crave Him and His strength (His might and inflexibility to temptation); seek and require His face and His presence [continually] evermore.

Psalm 105:3-4 (Amp)

Father God,

I take a few minutes this morning to think about Your power, Your sovereignty, Your holiness, Your glory. I am seeking You and all that You are. I ask only these things today: that as I seek You, You would open my mind to understand how I can put You first in my life and how I can live in Your Presence with more consistency. I do know that I need You each and every day. I thank You for this quiet time we are sharing together. I seek You and make these requests in Jesus' name.

Song Suggestion: Surrender *by* Jeremy Camp

March 23

Discouragement

That is why we never give up. Though our bodies are dying, our spirits are being renewed every day. For our present troubles are small and won't last very long. Yet they produce for us a glory that vastly outweighs them and will last forever! So we don't look at the troubles we can see now; rather, we fix our gaze on things that cannot be seen.
For the things we see now will soon be gone, but the things we cannot see will last forever.

2 Corinthians 4:16-18 (NLT)

Father God,

Thank You for Your Word that reminds me that all my disappointments, all my discouraging feelings are temporary. As I fix my eyes on You, I hold onto Your promises of life and love, and I meditate on these things. I replace my discouraging thoughts with thoughts of You and Your promises. You promise to meet all my needs as I trust in You. You promise to love me unconditionally and never leave me alone. You have a unique purpose for me. You are faithful. I believe You will guide me so that I will be able to rise above my self-pity and give me power and strength to keep going so that I can live for You. I thank You for Your power in my life. I thank You for renewing me. I thank You that my discouragement is temporary, and Your promises are eternal. In gratitude and with a hopeful heart, I pray in Jesus' name.

Song Suggestion: Rise Up *by* Third Day

March 24

God's Love

And I am convinced that nothing can ever separate us from God's love. Neither death nor life, neither angels nor demons, neither our fears for today nor our worries about tomorrow-not even the powers of hell can separate us from God's love. No power in the sky above or in the earth below-indeed, nothing in all creation will ever be able to separate us from the love of God that is revealed in Christ Jesus our Lord.

Romans 8:38-39 (NLT)

Father God,

I am thinking about Your love that surrounds me and fills me. Nothing I do can take away Your love. Neither can anyone else take Your love away from me. I thank You and praise You for Your infinite love. I sometimes forget that You are my loving Father. You are not keeping score of my good deeds and bad. You are not mad at me. You have shared Your only Son with me to save me and show me Your love. I let Your profound love soak into my whole being in this moment. I send my love and gratitude back to You this morning. I will honor You by sharing Your deep, unconditional love with others. In Jesus' good and holy name, I pray.

Song Suggestion: Nothing Ever Could Separate Us *by* Citizen Way

March 25

Hope

For whatever was written in earlier times was written for our instruction, so that through perseverance and the encouragement of the Scriptures we might have hope.

Romans 15:4 (NASB)

Father God,

Thank You for Your instruction book that has been written over thousands of years and is thousands of years old. Many would say it is 'antiquated' or 'old-fashioned', but I believe it is as vital now as when it was written. You have not changed. You still give us instructions. You still give me encouragement. You still give me hope -- hope that lives within me and gives me patience, kindness, optimism, and faith. I put all my hope in You, Father, Spirit, Jesus. I believe You are the hope of the world. I pray this in Jesus' name. Jesus, who is my living hope.

Song Suggestion: The Word is Alive *by* Casting Crowns

Perseverance

Moreover [let us also be full of joy now!] Let us exult and triumph in our troubles and rejoice in our sufferings, knowing that pressure and affliction and hardship produce patient and unswerving endurance. And endurance (fortitude) develops maturity of character (approved faith and tried integrity), and character [of this sort] produces [the habit of] joyful and confident hope of eternal salvation.

Romans 5:3-4 (Amp)

Father God,

Thank You that You know what is best for me. While I can only see what is in my line of vision, You can see the whole picture and know what I need, what is best for me.

Sometimes what I need is not what I want at all. When I am in a situation that is causing me suffering, hardship and/or pain, help me to remember that You are with me and if I keep moving forward while trusting You, praising You, serving You, then You will move me to a victory someway, somehow. You will use all the hard things that I go through for good. I will persevere. I will keep going, trusting You and knowing that You will not leave me. I put my hand in Yours today. In Jesus' name I pray.

Song Suggestion: Stand In Your Love *by* Josh Baldwin

March 27

I am a Child of God

Therefore, COME OUT FROM THEIR MIDST AND BE SEPARATE,*" says the Lord. "*AND DO NOT TOUCH WHAT IS UNCLEAN; *and I will welcome you. And I will be a father to you, and you shall be sons and daughters to Me," says the Lord Almighty.*

2 Corinthians 6:17-18 (NASB)

Father God,

This morning, I sit with You and declare that I believe. I believe that You are my God, my Father, my protector, my provider, my healer, my creator. I am so thankful that You are guiding me on this journey and teaching me Your ways. I close my eyes and picture You in all Your glory and majesty surrounded by angels praising You day and night. And yet, I can see You open Your arms to me with welcoming love saying, "You are my beloved child." And I am so humbled and in awe of Your grace, mercy, and love. I am so grateful that I am Your child. And so, Father, I give You my spirit and all that I am. I pray in Jesus' name this morning.

Song Suggestion: Who I Am *by* Ben Fuller

Motivation

But you, Timothy, are a man of God; so run from all these evil things. Pursue righteousness and a godly life, along with faith, love, perseverance, and gentleness. Fight the good fight for the true faith. Hold tightly to the eternal life to which God has called you, which you have confessed so well before many witnesses.

1 Timothy 6:11-12 (NLT)

Father God,

I believe that Your ways are the best ways, the right ways - the ways that will lead me to living an abundant, purpose filled, light infused life. I ask You today to help me stay motivated in pursuing goodness and godliness. Fill me with Your love, Your gentleness and a solid, immovable faith so that I can be a good model for others. I believe that You are changing me from the inside out ever so slowly. Thank You for guiding me and teaching me and gently pushing me in this fight. Thank You for calling me into a life of eternity starting right now. I pray this prayer in Jesus' name.

Song Suggestion: Light a Fire *by* David Leonard

March 29

Pray for Others

And in that day you will say: "Praise the LORD, call upon His name; Declare His deeds among the peoples, Make mention that His name is exalted.

Isaiah 12:4 (NKJV)

Father God,

I give You thanks for all You are and all You have done for me. I give You my heart filled with gratitude for my salvation. I take time this morning to think about others who may not know all the awesome things that You have done for all of us. I pray specifically for… (**Note**: *Pray, by name, for the people in your life who may not have a relationship with God*). I pray that they will learn and know of Your goodness and Your holiness, and I pray for their salvation. I pray that You will give me the courage to stand strong for You; to let others know of the love You have shown me. I thank You that You are continuing to show me Your way. I love You and exalt You and Your name above all. I pray in Jesus' name.

Song Suggestion: Prayer for a Friend *by* Casting Crowns

March 30

I am… The Temple of God

Do you not know that you are the temple of God and that the Spirit of God dwells in you. If anyone defiles the temple of God, God will destroy him. For the temple of God is holy, which temple you are.

1 Corinthians 3:16-17 (NKJV)

Father God,

You are such a mystery to me! Today I read that I am the temple of God and that You live in me. You say that I am holy. I read this and think, "You must mean someone else because I do not feel in any way holy." However, I will rely on Your Word and not on my feelings. I will ask You to help me every day to elevate my life (my thoughts, my words, my actions/behavior) so that Your temple is respected and holy. I believe that only You can make it so. I surrender to You today and lean on You as I gratefully live this day with You and for You. In Jesus' name I pray today.

Song Suggestion: Temple *by* Brandon Lake

March 31

I Will...

You know this, my beloved brothers and sisters. Now everyone must be quick to hear, slow to speak, and slow to anger;

James 1:19 (NASB)

Father God,

I praise You and thank You for always listening to me and that You are slow to get angry at me. Because of Your love, I want to obey You. I read today's scripture and recognize that the concepts that James is teaching are an area where I need to improve. A lot!

Therefore, I will be a good listener, on purpose. I will not have to make my point the most important part of a conversation. When I disagree with someone, I will listen with an open mind and respond with dignity and kindness. I will not be offended. I will try to give others a 'break' and/or the benefit of the doubt. I ask You to help me with these difficult tasks. And when I fail, the Holy Spirit will convict me (without condemning me), and I will ask for Your forgiveness, and You will help me try again. Thank You for Your patience with me. For You are slow to get angry with me! Thank You for staying faithful and staying by my side. I pray all these prayers today in Jesus' patient name.

Song Suggestion: I'm Listening *by* Chris McClarney

Holy, Sovereign God

All Your works shall praise You, O LORD, And Your saints shall bless You. They shall speak of the glory of Your kingdom, and talk of Your power, to make known to the sons of men His mighty acts, and the glorious majesty of His kingdom. Your kingdom is an everlasting kingdom, and Your dominion endures throughout all generations.

Psalm 145:10-13 (NKJV)

Father God,

This morning, I am taking some time to just think about all You have created, all Your works. I join Your believers in praising, blessing, and giving You glory. I acknowledge Your unfathomable power here on earth and in Your everlasting kingdom. Your power, Your glory, Your dominion will go on forever. It can be hard to see all of this in the world we live in today. In general, people think that they are in total control of most things in their lives. If I am honest, I often think that I am in control and I take control in any way I can. But right now, I declare that I am putting my faith in You as the one, true, mighty God. I put my life in Your hands as I pray today. I meditate on Your everlasting goodness and Your everlasting kingdom where You are my holy, sovereign Father God. Again, I will voice my praise to You, giving You the glory You deserve. In Jesus' name I pray.

Song Suggestion: How Great Thou Art *by* Carrie Underwood feat Vince Gill

April 2

Praise

Around midnight Paul and Silas were praying and singing hymns to God, and the other prisoners were listening. Suddenly, there was a massive earthquake, and the prison was shaken to its foundations. All the doors immediately flew open, and the chains of every prisoner fell off!

Acts 16:25-26 (NLT)

Father God,

I am so thankful that I can come to You and praise You even when things are not going my way. I am praising You now and I have faith that You hear me, and You are with me. I choose to praise You when things are going great, and I will praise You when they are not. I see from Paul and Silas that it is beneficial to give praise even in the hardest of times. Even when things are difficult in this life, You are still good. You are still holy. You are still my Father who has given me so many blessings and You continue to do so, even when I am blind to them. You are worthy to be praised and I take time this morning to focus on just praising You and giving You the honor, glory, admiration, and love that You deserve. In Jesus' name I pray today.

Song Suggestion: Paul and Silas (At Midnight) *by* Naomi Raine Feat Chandler Moore

April 3

Wisdom

For God gives wisdom and knowledge and joy to a man who is good in His sight; but to the sinner He gives the work of gathering and collecting that he may give to him who is good before God. This also is vanity and grasping for the wind.

Ecclesiastes 2:26 (NKJV)

Father God,

Thank You for all that You are - so loving, so kind, so good. You give wisdom, You give knowledge, You give joy to the ones who please You. As I strive to know You, to live like You and for You and as I grow in my learning, I open my whole self to You so that I may receive Your wisdom, knowledge, and joy. Like spiritual rain, I envision these gifts falling on me, around me and in me. I close my eyes and tilt my head to You and accept Your gifts with love, gratitude, praise, and a humble heart. Again, I thank You for continuing to do the patient work that You are doing in me. I will try every day to please You more and more. In Jesus' holy name I pray.

Song Suggestion: Center My Life *by* Austin Stone Worship

Forgiven

So repent (change your mind and purpose); turn around and return [to God], that your sins may be erased (blotted out, wiped clean), that times of refreshing (of recovering from the effect of heat, of reviving with fresh air) may come from the presence of the Lord;

Acts 3:19 (Amp)

Father God,

I come to You this morning with a desire to repent, to change my life so that I am living for You and doing things Your way and not my way. I ask You to help me with this every day. I place myself in your hands. I am asking for Your forgiveness for all the things that I have done that are contrary to Your will. I accept Your forgiveness. I am grateful that my sins can be wiped away, erased. I quiet myself now in Your holy and perfect Presence as You refresh my mind and my soul. With a heart full of gratitude and love, I pray in Jesus' merciful name this morning.

Song Suggestion: Come to the Altar *by* Elevation Worship

Open Ears

"Look! I stand at the door and knock. If you hear my voice and open the door, I will come in, and we will share a meal together as friends. Those who are victorious will sit with me on my throne, just as I was victorious and sat with my Father on his throne.

Revelations 3:20-21 (NLT)

Father God,

Thank You for trying to get my attention. Thank You for not giving up on me. Help me to hear You. Help me to understand You and Your ways. Help me to cooperate with You. I have so much to learn, and I know You will open doors for me to learn and You will open doors for me to serve You. I am knocking on Your door right now. I am opening my Spirit up to Yours as I sit quietly in Your Presence this morning. I am grateful for this quiet time we have together. Open my ears so that I will hear Your voice. Your voice alone. Open my eyes so that I will see You working in my life. I invite You in. I pray in Jesus' name today.

Song Suggestion: Open the Eyes of My Heart *by* Michael W. Smith

Joy

You love him even though you have never seen him. Though you do not see him now, you trust him; and you rejoice with a glorious, inexpressible joy. The reward for trusting him will be the salvation of your souls.

1 Peter 1:8-9 (NLT)

Father God,

I am reminded this Easter season that You are my salvation. I have faith in Jesus, and I believe, and I trust that Jesus has paid my sin debt, has redeemed me, and has saved me. As I meditate on this truth, I can invite and allow gratitude and joy to fill my heart, soul, and mind. I can sit with You and let Your light, Your victory, Your holy Presence surround me, enter me. We can share this wonderful joy together in this moment. I can carry this joy from trusting You for all my days. I pray with gratitude today in Jesus' name.

Song Suggestion: Rejoice *by* Chris Tomlin

April 7

Love God, Love Others

Some people are always greedy for more, but the godly love to give!

Proverbs 21:26 (NLT)

Father God,

You gave Your only son to die for me so I could be saved and adopted into Your family. Because of Your generosity, I am able to spend eternity with You surrounded by Your perfect love. You are a God who continues to give to me. Thank You for Your gifts. Help me let Your blessings flow through me to others. Open my eyes so that I can see people whom I can show Your love. Open my heart so that I have a passion and willingness to love others. Help me not only to pray for others but do something to show Your love. I will be Your light in this world. I love You Lord. In Jesus' name I pray.

Song Suggestion: Be a Light *by* Thomas Rhett, Reba McEntire and Chris Tomlin

April 8

Names of God

El ROI:

A Hebrew name of God meaning the God who sees me; God never sleeps. God is aware, He is the great Omnipresent God.

Thereafter, Hagar used another name to refer to the LORD, who had spoken to her. She said, "You are the God who sees me. She also said, "Have I truly seen the One who sees me?"

Genesis 16:13 (NLT)

Father God,

You are El Roi, the God who sees me. You are fully aware of all that concerns me. You know me inside and out. You know all my hopes, dreams, fears, the good and the bad. Still, You look on me with love, with understanding, with compassion. I thank You for Your constant love, Your constant mercy and kindness. I am filled with gratitude and love for You. I am in awe that such a powerful, omniscient, perfect, holy God would know me as I do not feel important enough. Thank You for looking down from Your throne in heaven to see me. Thank You, thank You that I have been given this knowledge so that I can choose to live my life for You, the one true God. In Jesus' name I pray this prayer today.

Song Suggestion: The God Who Sees *by* Doxa Church

Jesus

Therefore [because He stooped so low] God has highly exalted Him and has freely bestowed on Him the name that is above every name, that in (at) the name of Jesus every knee should (must) bow, in heaven and on earth and under the earth, and every tongue [frankly and openly] confess and acknowledge that Jesus Christ is Lord, to the glory of God the Father.

Philippians 2:9-11 (Amp)

Father God and Jesus,

Thank You for today. Thank You for the knowledge I have of Your truth. I believe that You are the one true God and Jesus You are the one and only Son. I believe that one day every knee will bow at Your holy name. I am not waiting but I am starting right now, in this moment. I bow down before You and declare that Your name is above every other name. You are the sovereign Lord, the living God. I look up to You and humbly submit to You my life. I rest in Your arms as I give glory to You Father God, to You Holy Spirit and to Jesus the one true King. I pray in Jesus' highly exalted name.

Song Suggestion: All Hail King Jesus *by* Jeremy Riddle

April 10

Eternity Minded

I saw no temple in the city, for the Lord God Omnipotent [Himself] and the Lamb [Himself] are its temple. And the city has no need of the sun nor of the moon to give light to it, for the splendor and radiance (glory) of God illuminate it, and the Lamb is its lamp. The nations shall walk by its light and the rulers and leaders of the earth shall bring into it their glory.

Revelation 21:22-24 (Amp)

Father God and Jesus,

You said that You are the light of the world. Right now, on earth, this is a spiritual reality. But in eternity, You are the actual light. There is no need for the sun or moon. This eternity that You have promised is hard for me to grasp. However, I am putting my faith and trust in You that all Your promises of heaven are true. I can imagine that eternity will be a glorious, light filled, love filled, beautiful place where all my needs are met. I will utterly be at peace. I am choosing to live my days, now on earth, remembering that I will eventually live eternally with You. I am choosing to live with You and for You today and every day. As I always do, I ask You to help me with this lofty plan. Jesus, I pray today in Your holy name.

Song Suggestion: On That Day (Live) *by* City Alight

Believing

For Jesus is the one referred to in the Scriptures, where it says, 'The stone that you builders rejected has now become the cornerstone.' There is salvation in no one else! God has given no other name under heaven by which we must be saved."

Acts 4:11-12 (NLT)

Jesus,

I believe that You are the One who saves. I believe that You are the cornerstone of my faith. Everything I believe is built on You and all You have done and all that You have taught. Back in the time when You lived, the religious people were offended by Your teachings, and they despised You and eventually put You to death. But Your Word along with Your message of hope, love, salvation, and eternal life rose with You and is still standing strong and firm today. You are my hope, Jesus. You are my salvation. And for that I praise You and thank You now and I will thank You and praise You forever more! I pray in Jesus' the Savior's name today.

Song Suggestion: Cornerstone *by* Hillsong Worship

April 12

Peace

Finally, brothers and sisters, rejoice, mend your ways, be comforted, be like-minded, live in peace; and the God of love and peace will be with you.

2 Corinthians 13:11 (NASB)

Father God,

I believe that You are the God of love and peace. Help me live joyfully as I walk with You each day. Help me live peacefully with You and with those around me. Holy Spirit, show me how to think, act and react in peaceful ways. I am so grateful that You are with me, every moment on this journey. I am comforted knowing that I am never alone. I can lean on You always and You will hold me in Your arms. I can close my eyes and fall into Your arms and be enveloped in Your love and peace. I am closing my eyes in this moment, inviting Your Presence in. Continue to help me walk closely with You in harmonious and tranquil ways. I praise You and thank You for Your consistent, unfailing, faithful love and care for me. I pray in Jesus' peaceful name.

Song Suggestion: Perfect Peace *by* Laura Story

God's Will

Now may the God of peace- who brought up from the dead our Lord Jesus, the great Shepherd of the sheep, and ratified an eternal covenant with his blood- May he equip you with all you need for doing his will. May he produce in You, through the power of Jesus Christ, every good thing that is pleasing to him. All glory to him forever and ever! Amen.

Hebrews 13:20-21 (NLT)

Father God,

Thank You for equipping me to do Your will. Thank You for giving me strength to do good things. I am asking the Holy Spirit right now to show me someone who needs God's love today. Holy Spirit, tell me exactly what I need to do and give me the courage and the determination to do it. I know that You will give me the power I need to do what you want me to do. If I see someone with a need, I will do my best to fill it. Help me every day to be Your light, Your hands, Your feet. By serving You, I give You glory. All glory is Yours now and forever. In Jesus' name I pray today.

Song Suggestion: Christ in Me *by* Jeremy Camp

April 14

Thoughts/Mindset

So brace up your minds; be sober (circumspect, morally alert); set your hope wholly and unchangeably on the grace (divine favor) that is coming to you when Jesus Christ (the Messiah) is revealed.

1 Peter 1:13 (Amp)

Father God,

Your Word tells me to prepare my mind so that I am morally alert and to fix my hope on Your grace. Oh, how I need You, how I need Your help! I start now by soaking myself in Your holy and living Presence this morning. I think about all the promises that You have given me. I think about all the favor and grace that You have shown me despite all my shortcomings. I think about all the ways that You are helping me in this life. I think about all Your goodness and mercy. I ask You to show me when my thinking becomes ungodly, selfish, or uncaring. Help me to rid myself of these thoughts and replace them with thoughts that are wholesome and helpful. Holy Spirit, I ask You to open my mind to Your thoughts. I praise You and thank You for Your grace that is pouring over me now and will continue to until Jesus comes. I pray today in Jesus' name.

Song Suggestion: Still My Mind *by* Destiny Worship Music

April 15

The Presence of God

But it is good for me to draw near to God; I have put my trust in the Lord God and made Him my refuge, that I may tell of all Your works.

Psalm 73:28 (Amp)

Father God,

This morning, I am drawing near to You. I am sitting in Your Presence, slowing down, becoming still. I am putting aside all distractions so that I may focus on You and only You. You are the Lord over my life, even though I often forget this and go down my own path. I am declaring that I will put my trust in You. I know that as I put my worries, my family, my whole life into Your hands then I can let go and live in a more peaceful and joyful way. As I make You my refuge, I can relax and give up the idea that I am in control. I can thank You that You are working on my behalf, and I can rest. As my day progresses and I start to get busy and unraveled, remind me to draw close to You again. As I learn to live in Your Presence more and more, I will become a better version of myself with You by my side. Thank You for working with me and guiding me back to You every day. I pray in Jesus' name.

Song Suggestion: Holy Spirit *by* Francesca Battistelli

April 16

Trust God

This hope is a strong and trustworthy anchor for our souls. It leads us through the curtain into God's inner sanctuary.

Hebrews 6:19 (NLT)

Father God,

This morning, I am meditating on You as my anchor of hope. I envision myself like a boat that is anchored to You. As waves of challenges and troubles come my way, I am thankful I have You to hold on to. I ask the Holy Spirit to help me increase my innermost faith so that I will purposefully think about You as my sincere hope. I trust that You are with me. You are taking my hand as I place my hand in Yours in perfect trust and although my troubles are not disappearing, You are giving me strength and power to overcome them. You will enable me to overcome all my circumstances and difficulties as I trust in, hope in, and obey You. I praise You, thank You and give You the glory for being the one true God who I can place all my hope and trust in. I pray this prayer in Jesus' name today.

Song Suggestion: Stay Strong *by* Danny Gokey

Forgiving

Then Peter came to Him and said "Lord, how often shall my brother sin against me, and I forgive him? Up to seven times?" Jesus said to him, "I do not say to you, up to seven times, but up to seventy times seven.

Matthew 18:21-22 (NKJV)

Father God,

You are the One Who forgives. Thank You for teaching me about forgiveness. Thank You that I can live in the freedom that mercy and forgiveness provide. Because You have forgiven me, Father, Jesus instructs me to forgive others who sin against me, who hurt me, who disappoint me, who betray me. And when I learn to do this, I am free from being offended. I am free to live in peace, harmony, and tranquility. I am free from anger and living a bitter, negative, oppressed life. I can forgive repeatedly with Your help.

Thank You for helping me. Thank You that I can depend on You when forgiveness seems unreasonable, unattainable and/or unfair. I am depending on You, Holy Spirit, to walk me through the challenging times when forgiveness seems impossible. I will decide to forgive others and I will lean on You to do so. I pray this prayer in Jesus' name.

Song Suggestion: Where Forgiveness Is *by* Sidewalk Prophets

April 18

My Words

Let no foul or polluting language, nor evil word nor unwholesome or worthless talk [ever] come out of your mouth, but only such [speech] as is good and beneficial to the spiritual progress of others, as is fitting to the need and the occasion, that it may be a blessing and give grace (God's favor) to those who hear it.

Ephesians 4:29 (Amp)

Father God,

I am so, so grateful that You give me encouragement so that I can be a blessing to others. I am grateful that You have given me the ability to have self-control when it comes to using my words. Although I am inconsistent, even lacking, in this area, I am committed to learning and improving. Right now, I dedicate my mouth to You. I will think before I speak. I am slowing my pace right now to think about the value of words and what it is You want from me in this area. I am deciding right now to use my words to encourage and build up others. I am going to be a blessing to others because I have control over what I say. I am asking the Holy Spirit to help me today. Holy Spirit, be my mentor, my guide, my teacher. I am thanking You and praising You along with my holy Father and loving Savior, Jesus. I am especially grateful for Your patience with me as I work on controlling what I say. I pray and ask for Your help in Jesus' name.

Song Suggestion: I Speak Jesus *by* Charity Gayle feat. Steven Musso

April 19

Anxiety

Cast your burden upon the Lord *and He will sustain you; He will never allow the righteous to be shaken.*

Psalm 55:22 (NASB)

Father God,

I come to You this morning with deep gratitude that You are a God who listens to me and cares about every little and important thing in my life. Today I am casting my burdens on You. I am feeling overwhelmed with... (**Note**: *Communicate your worries, thoughts, problems to God*). I am placing all these issues/problems/feelings in Your hands. I am letting them go. I believe that You will sustain me, You will uphold me even as situations get difficult. You "have my back" and I am so grateful. I am allowing myself to be filled with joy and hope because I can trust and depend on You to strengthen me. I take time right now to breathe in Your joy, breathe in Your peace, breathe in Your hope. I know that I may not have every prayer answered exactly as I would like - but You will get me through all things as I lean on You. I praise You and worship You through all my good times, and all my anxious times. I pray this prayer with gratitude in Jesus' name.

Song Suggestion: Give Me Your Peace (Live) *by* Gateway Worship

Thankful

We also pray that you will be strengthened with all his glorious power so you will have all the endurance and patience you need. May you be filled with joy, always thanking the Father. He has enabled you to share in the inheritance that belongs to his people, who live in the light.

Colossians 1:11-12 (NLT)

Father God,

I am so thankful for Your power in my life. Even though I do not always feel it, I have faith that You are strengthening me and helping me each day. I believe that You will give me the endurance and patience I need to live my life in a positive and godly way. You have also blessed me with an inheritance. I am so thankful that I can look forward to an eternity of living with You in Your perfect and beautiful light and love. I am thanking You now for these gifts. I am letting the thought of being in Your Presence flow into my mind and soul which brings me peace, hope and joy. You are THE God of blessings, and I am forever grateful and will praise You for all my days. In Jesus' name I pray today.

Song Suggestion: Father I Thank You *by* Jeremy Camp, Adrienne Camp

Prayer

Yes, the Almighty will be your gold And your precious silver; for then you will have your delight in the Almighty, and lift up your face to God. You will make your prayer to Him, He will hear you, and you will pay your vows. You will also declare a thing, and it will be established for you; so light will shine on your ways.

Job 22:25-28 (NKJV)

Father God,

I am lifting my face up to You this morning. I am wanting to put You first in every area of my life. I want to build my life around You. Of course, what I want and what I do can be different and so I come to You solemnly asking You to help me in this area. Lead me and guide me. I am so grateful that Your light will shine down upon me. I believe that You hear my prayers, and You will answer me. I believe in You, almighty Father. Continue to shine on me as I try to shine for You. In Jesus' name I come to you and pray today.

Song Suggestion: On My Knees *by* Jaci Valasquez

April 22

Seek God

"so that they should seek the Lord, in the hope that they might grope for Him and find Him, though He is not far from each one of us; "for in Him we live and move and have our being, as also some of your own poets have said, 'For we are also His offspring.'

Acts 17:27-28 (NKJV)

Father God,

In my busy life, I sometimes wonder where You are. Today's scripture tells me that if I seek You, just grasp for You, You can be found. You are not far from me. Therefore, this morning I quiet my mind and my thoughts, and I breathe in and out and quiet my body as I seek You. I accept that You are here with me. I can praise You, thank You, and tell You anything that is on my mind. I have faith that You are my Father who listens to me and looks on me with love, for I am Your child. I thank You for our time together and I ask You to help me to seek Your Presence all throughout my day. In Jesus' name I pray.

Song Suggestion: Crowns Down *by* Gateway Worship feat Josh Baldwin

Discouragement

For I the Lord your God hold your right hand; I am the Lord, Who says to you, Fear not; I will help you!

Isaiah 41:13 (Amp)

Father God,

When I am disappointed and discouraged by all that this life throws at me, I am so deeply grateful that I know You, that You are my Lord and my God. I am taking time right now to rest in You. I am remembering that You are holding my hand. I don't always feel that way, but I know by faith that You are carrying me, and You are leading me and helping me. I do not need to be fearful, depressed, anxious, bitter, or angry. I am letting all these negative feelings go. I am grasping for Your (spiritual) hand and sitting quietly, basking in Your love. I intentionally remember that You are good to me, even in challenging times. I am giving You thanks and praise for being so good to me no matter what is going on in my life. In Jesus' name I pray this morning.

Song Suggestion: Help is on the Way *by* Michael W. Smith

April 24

God's Love

That He would grant you, according to the riches of His glory, to be strengthened with might through His Spirit in the inner man, that Christ may dwell in your hearts through faith; that you, being rooted and grounded in love, may be able to comprehend with all the saints what is the width and length and depth and height - to know the love of Christ which passes knowledge; that you may be filled with all the fullness of God.

Ephesians 3:16-19 (NKJV)

Father God,

My prayer today is straight out of the apostle Paul's letter to the Ephesians. I ask that You strengthen me and my loved ones with power through Your Holy Spirit. I pray that Jesus continues to live in our hearts through our faith. I ask You to empower us so that we are rooted and grounded in love; help us understand how deep and true Your love is. Open our eyes to know Your love, to really, really, deeply have faith in our hearts and minds that Your love is true and belongs to us. And I ask that You fill us with the fullness of You, Father, Spirit, and Jesus. I pause and think about these things today. I pray this prayer with admiration, praise, and gratitude, in Jesus' name.

Song Suggestion: Love of God *by* MercyMe

April 25

Hope

By having the eyes of your heart flooded with light, so that you can know and understand the hope to which He has called you, and how rich is His glorious inheritance in the saints (His set-apart ones),

Ephesians 1:18 (Amp)

Father God,

I pray this prayer over myself and my family and friends. I pray that You will flood the eyes of our hearts with Your light so that we can know and understand more of You. Help us to know and understand Your love and the hope that You have given us. Oh, help us to comprehend what it means to receive Your glorious inheritance. Especially when I consider how undeserving we are and what a gift this is. I reach for Your light, for more knowledge and experience of You and Your ways. You are our true hope. You are our only hope. I pray in Jesus' name today.

Song Suggestion: Living Hope *by* Phil Wickham

Perseverance

And you will be hated by all for My name's sake, but he who perseveres and endures to the end will be saved [from spiritual disease and death in the world to come].

Matthew 10:22 (Amp)

Jesus,

While You were here on earth, too many people turned away from You. Leaders hatefully plotted to kill You, but Your death and resurrection blessed us with the accounts of Your amazing fortitude and perseverance. Your life story is the rock I build my faith upon. Help me stand strong in my belief, knowing that I am Your faithful follower. There may be people who reject me or even hate me because I follow You, but I will proclaim Your sacrifice on the Cross. Guide me so that I will keep my focus on You habitually.

Thank You for Your promises which continually give me hope and confidence no matter what others think or say. I belong to You, and I pray that I will persevere in living my life Your way in a skeptical world that does not understand. I pray today in Jesus' holy name.

Song Suggestion: Take Courage (Radio Version) *by* Kristene DiMarco

April 27

I am a Child of God

For the LORD will not abandon His people on account of His great name, because the LORD has been pleased to make you a people for Himself.

1 Samuel 12:22 (NASB)

Father God,

Thank You for sending Jesus so that through Him, I can be adopted into Your family. Because I am Your son/daughter, You will never abandon me. You are with me through all my difficulties, you show me mercy and love when I am spiritually far away from You. Help me not to take this beautiful, priceless, precious gift of being Your child for granted. I am taking that reality into my mind, heart, and soul in this moment. I am slowing down this morning to allow this promise to flourish within me. Help me to live my life because You love and cherish me. I pray in the holy name of Jesus today.

Song Suggestion: Still Calls Me Son *by* John Waller

April 28

Motivation

And as for you, brethren, do not become weary or lose heart in doing right [but continue in well-doing without weakening].

2 Thessalonians 3:13 (Amp)

Father God,

Thank you that there are so many good believers in this world. While evil is abundant in our world today, Your glory, Your beauty, Your goodness and Your kindness abound still. Let my daily purpose be to bring Your light and Your goodness to all those around me. I set my intention to encourage others, to be a blessing, to fill needs that I see, to help others. Sometimes (often), living this way will be inconvenient or costly. May the Holy Spirit help me power through. May the Holy Spirit keep me from giving up. May the Holy Spirit give me Your wisdom, Your energy, Your generosity to keep me motivated to do Your will. Help me be Your love, Your hands, Your feet, and Your voice today and every day. In Jesus' name I pray.

Song Suggestion: Made to Worship *by* Chris Tomlin

April 29

Pray for Others

And I will give them singleness of heart and put a new spirit within them. I will take away their stony, stubborn heart, so they will obey My decrees and regulations. Then they will truly be my people and I will be their God.

Ezekiel 11:19-20 (NLT)

Father God,

Thank You for all the chances that You have given me. I am so thankful that You have given me a new spirit, a renewed spirit and a new heart that belongs to You. I know people who do not have this new heart and new Spirit. I am praying now for … (**Note**: *Tell God those people on your heart for whom to pray*). I am asking You to give them a new heart and a new spirit as well so that together we may be a part of Your family and together we can praise You now and forever. I will keep praying for (*names*) and I thank You that You are working in all our lives. I pray in Jesus' name.

Song Suggestion: Let the Worshippers Arise *by* Phillips, Craig and Dean

I am... Confident

The LORD directs the steps of the godly. He delights in every detail of their lives. Though they stumble, they will never fall, for the LORD holds them by the hand.

Psalm 37:23-24 (NLT)

Father God,

Thank You for directing my steps. I ask that You give me wisdom in every detail, small and big, in my life. I am grateful that You want to be involved in all the details in my life. I know that, although I try very hard to do things Your way, I often fall short. I often do not understand the big picture, or I just don't know what to do. I am so grateful that when I mess up, You hold me by the hand. I can live confidently because You are helping me, guiding me on the journey, You are with me to help me get back on track whenever I misstep. You make me brave and confident. Thank You for all Your protection and provision. I pray with gratitude and praise to my Father in Jesus' name.

Song Suggestion: You Make Me Brave *by* Amanda Cook and Bethel Music

May 1

Holy, Sovereign God

After that I heard what sounded like the shout of a vast throng, like the boom of many pounding waves, and like the roar of terrific and mighty peals of thunder, exclaiming, Hallelujah (praise the Lord)! For now the Lord our God the Omnipotent (the All-Ruler) reigns!

Revelation 19:6 (Amp)

Father God,

You are our living God ruling over us forever. You are on Your throne, so far above me, yet somehow You are living with me, right beside me. People have turned away from You for lots of reasons. As they go their own way, without You, they lose Your help, Your blessings, Your hope. I choose to be different. I choose to seek You and honor You and live for You remembering that I belong to You. Hallelujah! Thank You Father for watching over me as I run to You, the almighty reigning God. I take time this morning to meditate on how holy You are, how mighty You are. I declare that You are reigning now and will reign forever more. You deserve all the honor and praise. In gratitude, I pray in Jesus' name.

Song Suggestion: Revelation Song *by* Kari Jobe

Praise

I will extol You, my God, O King; and I will bless Your name forever and ever [with grateful, affectionate praise]. Every day [with its new reasons] will I bless You [affectionately and gratefully praise You]; yes, I will praise Your name forever and ever. Great is the Lord and highly to be praised; and His greatness is [so vast and deep as to be] unsearchable.

Psalm 145:1-3 (Amp)

Father God,

This morning, I sit quietly in Your Presence, and I think about Your deep love, Your kindness, Your mercy. I think about today and all the wonderful reasons that I praise You! I take this time to thank You that I belong to You, the King, the one true God. You make today new. You give new mercy to me every morning. You deserve all my praise. Your Word tells me repeatedly about how great You are. I cannot really wrap my mind around how amazing, how awesome You truly are. Open my eyes to see Your glory.

Open my mind to comprehend more each day. Today and all days, I will bless You with affection and gratitude; I will praise and honor You. I will praise You, Lord, with all that is within me. In Jesus' name, I pray.

Song Suggestion: O Praise the Name (Anastasis) *by* Hillsong Worship

May 3

Wisdom

To acquire wisdom is to love oneself; people who cherish understanding will prosper.

Proverbs 19:8 (NLT)

Father God,

You are such a good Father that You want me to live successfully in my spiritual life and prosper in all areas of my life. Thank You for Your Word which teaches me Your wisdom and Your truth. Thank You for helping me to understand Your ways, even when they are contradictory to the world's ways. I continue to ask You to help me gain wisdom and understanding. I ask You to put people, ideas, books, songs, whatever it takes, in my life so that I will gain more of Your wisdom. I will intentionally seek to have a teachable attitude. And when I prosper in any area in my life, I will look to You with a humble and thankful heart because I know all good things come from You! I pray with a seeking and grateful heart in Jesus' name.

Song Suggestion: All the Way My Savior Leads Me *by* Chris Tomlin

Forgiven

But He was wounded for our transgressions, He was bruised for our guilt and iniquities; the chastisement [needful to obtain] peace and well-being for us was upon Him, and with the stripes [that wounded] Him we are healed and made whole.

Isaiah 53:5 (Amp)

Jesus,

I sit quietly and think about what You did for me and all others who believe. How can I ever thank You enough for being wounded, crushed, punished for me, so that I can be forgiven? Thank You for giving Your life for me. Thank You for taking away my shame, guilt, and punishment. You are my hope for the future. You are my Savior. I will forever be thankful and in debt to You. I will be forever Yours. I pray with deep praise, worship, honor, and gratitude in Your holy, worthy, saving name today.

Song Suggestion: By His Wounds *by* Mac Powell

May 5

Open Ears

Jesus replied, "But even more blessed are all who hear the word of God and put it into practice."

Luke 11:28 (NLT)

Father God,

I come to You this morning with a need for You. I want to do Your will, but I often get caught up in tasks and diversions, forgetting about You. I admit that I do not spend enough time with You or spend enough time studying Your Word. The noise and distractions in this world tend to draw me away from You. This morning, I ask You to reawaken a yearning in me for You. I ask You to open my ears to You. I want to know You and know Your heart. I want to please You. Open my heart, mind, and soul to Your Spirit. Lead me in the ways I should go. Right now, in this moment, I humble myself before You and ask You to help me clarify my intentions. Give me the tenacious spirit I need to follow You. In Jesus' name I ask these things.

Song Suggestion: We Are Listening *by* Steven Curtis Chapman

Joy

Now may the God of hope fill you with all joy and peace in believing, so that you will abound in hope by the power of the Holy Spirit.

Romans 15:13 (NASB)

Father God,

Thank You for filling me with Your spiritual gifts of hope, joy, and peace. Without Your Presence in my life, I would run out of faith pretty quickly. I ask You, Holy Spirit, to continue to fill me to overflowing with Your hope, with Your joy, with Your peace and with a confident, growing faith. I place my faith and trust in You right now. I take a minute to think about this faith that gives me so many positive blessings in my life. I live gratefully for the seeds of faith that You have planted in me. I can see, little by little, this faith blossoming. I can see the power of the Holy Spirit at work in my life. And I pray with a joyful attitude in Jesus' name today.

Song Suggestion: Rejoice *by* Andrew Ripp

May 7

Love God, Love Others

We know how much God loves us, and we have put our trust in his love. God is love, and all who live in love live in God, and God lives in them. And as we live in God, our love grows more perfect. So we will not be afraid on the day of judgment, but we can face him with confidence because we live like Jesus here in this world.

1 John 4:16-17 (NLT)

Father God,

I thank You and praise You for Your deep, unrelenting, unshakeable love for me. You are continually filling me with Your love. I want so much to follow Your loving ways. I ask You to help me be Your love in this world. I have faith that You will continue to help me as I can do nothing without You. Thank You for loving me, even though I am not perfect. You know that I am growing in love as I grow closer to You. Thank You for allowing me to share in Your love and to share in the giving of Your love to others. I set my purpose to live like Jesus so that I can face You with confidence today and in the future. Thank You Jesus, for being such an awesome example of how to live with compassion, mercy, and kindness. I pray today in Jesus' name.

Song Suggestion: One Life to Love *by* 33 Miles

Names of God

Jehovah Jireh

Abraham gave this name to the Lord to signify that God will provide.

Then Abraham lifted his eyes and looked, and there behind him was a ram caught in a thicket by its horns. So Abraham went and took the ram, and offered it up for a burnt offering instead of his son. And Abraham called the name of the place, The-LORD-Will-Provide, as it is said to this day, "In the Mount of the LORD it shall be provided."

Genesis 22:13-14 (NKJV)

Father God,

You are Jehovah Jireh, the One who provides. Thank You for providing for me. Thank You for all You have given me - my breath, my parents, my family, my loved ones. Thank You for the daily provisions that I often take for granted: food, home, water. Thank You for giving me work to do. Thank You for providing for me on a spiritual level and giving me faith, a faith that is always growing. You have given me Jesus. Through Jesus, I have become Your child. You give me peace, patience, kindness, guidance, love, joy, peace, hope and eternal life. You are my provider, and I will be grateful forever. I love You and praise You now, my providing Lord. In Jesus' name I pray today.

Song Suggestion: Jireh *by* Elevation Worship and Maverick City

Jesus

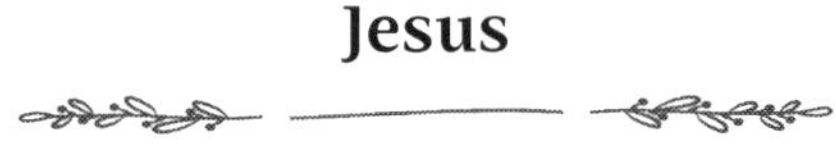

Jesus told her, "I am the resurrection and the life. Anyone who believes in me will live, even after dying. Everyone who lives in me and believes in me will never ever die. Do you believe this, Martha?"

John 11:25-26 (NLT)

Jesus,

Thank You for coming to this earth that You created. Thank You for showing us the love of the Father. Thank You for all You do for me. Thank You for sharing Your life with me. You expand my life and freely give me unconditional love, mercy, forgiveness, and freedom. I am choosing to live a life filled with love for You and love for others. I am choosing to remember how You have forgiven me and shown mercy to me over and over showing me how I can do the same. I believe in You Jesus, and I believe that what You said is true. You ARE the resurrection and the life. Because I live in and believe in You, I will never die. I will live with You in heaven for eternity. You have given me this gift, this hope. I am forever grateful. And I take time this morning to think about this amazing, life altering hope that You have provided. I praise You and I honor You and I give You all that I am today. In Your holy name I pray.

Song Suggestion: Resurrection Power *by* Chris Tomlin

Eternity Minded

All praise to God, the Father of our Lord Jesus Christ. It is by his great mercy that we have been born again, because God raised Jesus Christ from the dead. Now we live with great expectation, and we have a priceless inheritance - an inheritance that is kept in heaven for you, pure and undefiled, beyond the reach of change and decay. And through your faith, God is protecting you by his power until you receive this salvation, which is ready to be revealed on the last day for all to see.

1 Peter 1:3-5 (NLT)

Father God,

I am joining Peter in praising You today. I am also thanking You because You have promised to give me an inheritance, You have reserved a place in heaven for me. I have done nothing to earn it - You have given me this gift because I believe and I follow Your only son, Jesus. Not only have You given me salvation, but You are protecting and shielding me right now. You are my protector and my shield. How can I thank You for such awe-inspiring things? I set an intention today to allow Your Holy Spirit to work through me to help me live for You as an act of gratitude. I honor You for all You have done for me. I want to show You my love in the way that I live. I pray with deep gratitude in Jesus' name today.

Song Suggestion: Ain't No Grave *by* Bethel Music and Molly Skaggs

Believing

Jesus said to him, "If you can believe, all things are possible to him who believes." Immediately the father of the child cried out and said with tears, "Lord, I believe; help my unbelief!"

Mark 9:23-24 (NKJV)

Father God,

Thank You that You know me and my heart. You know that I believe but my belief often wavers depending on my circumstances. I am so grateful that You are willing to work with me and cover my limitations. This event in scripture is so beautiful because it shows how compassionate and kind You are. It shows that I can come to You with my weaknesses, with my doubt, with my lack of faith. I can come to You just as I am, and You will listen and put out Your hand to lift me higher. How loving, faithful, caring! And, You forgive my shortcomings in all these things. You are an amazing God! You are a perfect Father! You continue working with me to grow my belief and nurture my positive behaviors! I am so thankful that You are my God. I am thankful that Jesus is my Savior. I ask that You continue to decrease my unbelief and enrich my experiences of You in all areas in my life. I pray this in Jesus' name today.

Song Suggestion: I Still Believe *by* Jeremy Camp

Peace

In peace I will both lie down and sleep, for You, Lord, alone make me dwell in safety and confident trust.

Psalm 4:8 (Amp)

Father God,

Oh, how I need to trust in You rather than in myself and in my circumstances. For You are my provider - You give me all that I need. You alone take care of me. I can bless You at the end of each day because You give me breath and life all day long. You have provided for me, and I relinquish all my control over all my circumstances. I give all to You. As I trust You more, my heart, my mind, and my body fill with Your peace, Your rest, and Your tranquility. I am taking this opportunity right now to sit quietly and calm my mind and body. I am purposefully thinking about and breathing in Your perfect peace right now. As Your peace surrounds me, I let it saturate my soul. I am so grateful for Your gift of peace. Help me to remember that this peace is always within me. Thank You for giving me these opportunities to trust You more and to let Your peace rule in my heart and in my life. I pray this prayer in gratitude and love, in Jesus' name.

Song Suggestion: It Is Well With My Soul *by* Anthem Lights

May 13

God's Will

Your word is a lamp to my feet and a light to my path.

Psalm 119:105 (NASB)

Father God,

I come to You to ask You to ignite in me a passion to discover Your ways, Your truth, Your plans, Your vision and Your will for me by reading Your Holy Word. I make many excuses for why I do not put in the time to learn of You. However, I do want to get to know You more. I want to hear from You. I want to know Your will for me. I am asking You to create a yearning in me so that I will be persuaded to read, study, and meditate on Your Word. Thank You for Your Word which gives me light so that I know to stay on Your path. Thank You for all You do for me and all You have done and continue to do. I give You thanks and praise in this moment. I pray In Jesus' name today.

Song Suggestion: Your Word *by* Hillsong Worship

Thoughts/Mindset

And be constantly renewed in the spirit of your mind [having a fresh mental and spiritual attitude], and put on the new nature (the regenerate self) created in God's image, [Godlike] in true righteousness and holiness.

Ephesians 4:23-24 (Amp)

Father God,

This morning, I come to You with the intention of renewing my mind. I will try to do my part and ask You to do the rest. I imagine that I am spiritually sitting before Your throne. You are holy, perfect, wrapped in majesty and light. I bow humbly before You. I remember that You have given Your Son so that I can come before You now. I feel Your unconditional love and the joy that You have in sharing this time together. I ask that You renew my mind, my attitude. Help me to remember that You are my creator and You created me in Your image. Help me to have an attitude of gratitude and service. Let my thoughts, attitudes, and actions be purposeful with the intention of pleasing You. I love You Father, and I am eternally thankful that You help me in many ways, especially in helping me keep a holy, humble, joyful, grateful mindset. I invite You to stream Your thoughts into my mind all day long. I take time to just breathe in Your Presence right now. I pray this prayer with such deep gratitude in Jesus' name.

Song Suggestion: This Life *by* MercyMe

May 15

The Presence of God

Humble yourselves [feeling very insignificant] in the presence of the Lord, and He will exalt you [He will lift you up and make your lives significant].

James 4:10 (Amp)

Father God,

I come before You this morning with the recognition that I am nothing without You. I cannot do anything significant without You. I need more of You and less of me in my thoughts, attitudes, and actions. Your ways are the best ways. Your ways are perfect even though I often do not always truly understand all Your truth and all Your ways. Help me become more aware of Your Presence. It is in Your Presence where You are revealed. I realize more and more that I need You, I need Your holy and living Presence in my life to walk with me, to guide me, to steady me, to keep me on Your path - the path that You have laid out for me. In this moment, I am taking time to sit quietly with You. I am filled with worship, love, and praise. In Jesus' name I pray.

Song Suggestion: Nothing Else *by* Cody Carnes and The Belonging Co

May 16

Trust God

The LORD also will be a refuge for the oppressed, a refuge in times of trouble. And those who know Your name will put their trust in You; for You, LORD, have not forsaken those who seek You.

Psalm 9:9-10 (NKJV)

Father God,

Today I put out my hand to You and I know that You are taking it. I put my hand in Yours and decide that I will trust You with confidence, joy, and peace. You will not leave me now or ever as You will stay with me no matter what comes or no matter what I feel. I believe in You Father. I believe You are my protector, my provider, my healer. You make a way when there is no way. Even when undesirable and troublesome circumstances come my way, I trust you with the impossible. Thank You for all You have done, are doing and will continue to do in my life as I hold Your hand. I praise and thank You now and forever. In Jesus' name I pray.

Song Suggestion: Power *by* Chris Tomlin feat. Bear Rinehart

Forgiving

"And whenever you stand praying, if you have anything against anyone, forgive him, that your Father in heaven may also forgive you your trespasses. But if you do not forgive, neither will your Father in heaven forgive your trespasses."

Mark 11:25-26 (NKJV)

Father God,

I start my prayer time today thanking You for Your Word which is hard to hear in this scripture. I read that if I am angry at anyone or am holding a grudge against someone, I should forgive them, and live in peace. So, this morning I am thinking about ... (**Note**: *Communicate to God the names of people who you may need to forgive and the circumstances that led you to be offended, angry, annoyed, or hurt*). I am choosing to forgive (*names*). I will seek to walk in peace and love with (*names*) and with everyone around me. I will forgive others no matter what because You know what is best and You have commanded it. You have and You will continue to forgive me as a result. I am eternally grateful for Your unending mercy and patience with me. Help me to give mercy and patience to others. Thank You Father, Holy Spirit, and Jesus. In Jesus' name I pray today.

Song Suggestion: Everything & Nothing Else *by* Chris McClarney

My Words

May the words of my mouth and the meditation of my heart be acceptable in Your sight, Lord, my rock and my Redeemer.

Psalm 19:14 (NASB)

Father God,

Let this scripture, this prayer from Your holy Word, go straight from my heart and lips to You. I am asking You to help me control my words so that everything I say is pleasing to You. Let Your words be in my heart. Oh, I need Your help. I need You to stop me when I am going to say something that I should not and put encouraging, helpful words in my mind and mouth instead. Help me learn to have better control of my words. I take time this morning to consider that I have a choice in what I say and how I say it. I am learning that these lessons are extremely difficult to put into practice and maintain with consistency. However, I will not give up. I will ask You again and again to forgive me when I speak in a way that is displeasing to You and then I will try again! Thank You for your help and guidance. Thank You for being my rock on whom I can depend. Thank You for being my redeemer, You continually restore me. In Jesus' name I pray today.

Song Suggestion: Alive & Breathing *by* Matt Maher

May 19

Anxiety

Fear not [there is nothing to fear], for I am with you; do not look around you in terror and be dismayed, for I am your God. I will strengthen and harden you to difficulties, yes, I will help you; yes, I will hold you up and retain you with My [victorious] right hand of rightness and justice.

Isaiah 41:10 (Amp)

Father God,

You are the Lord who helps me in all situations. This morning, I am leaning into You. I am exchanging my fear for Your strength. I am exchanging my helplessness for Your power and Your guidance. I am taking hold of Your hand so that You can hold me up. I slow down and think about how You are holding me up right now in this moment. You are the one, true, powerful, almighty God who takes my hand as I stretch it out to You. I am soaking up all that You offer to share with me - Your peace, love, joy, hope. You are light over darkness. You are hope and peace over anxiety and depression. You are tranquil in chaos. My anxieties and worries disappear in Your Presence. And I am so, so grateful to You. I pray in deep adoration in Jesus' name.

Song Suggestion: I Will Carry You *by* Ellie Holcomb

May 20

Thankful

For though I am absent in the flesh, yet I am with you in spirit, rejoicing to see your good order and the steadfastness of your faith in Christ. As you therefore have received Christ Jesus the Lord, so walk in Him, rooted and built up in Him and established in the faith, as you have been taught, abounding in it with thanksgiving.

Colossians 2:5-7 (NKJV)

Father God,

Thank You for giving me faith. I have faith that I can do what I need to do as You make me braver, stronger, wiser. You help me be more loving, more compassionate. I believe that You will continue to make my life path clearer and give me endurance and patience. All these gifts come from being rooted and built up in You. I thank You for this faith. I thank You for all the seen and unseen blessings in my life. As I live each day, I intentionally choose to be thankful for everything in my life. All my gratitude is directed to You my heavenly Father, and to Jesus, my Savior and friend and to the Holy Spirit, my spiritual teacher, guide, and comforter. I do not know where I would be or how I would cope with life's challenges without my faith in You. I pray all these things in Jesus' name today.

Song Suggestion: I Thank God *by* Housefires

Prayer

Is anyone among you suffering? Let him pray. Is anyone cheerful? Let him sing psalms.

16 Confess your trespasses to one another, and pray for one another, that you may be healed. The effective, fervent prayer of the righteous man avails much.

James 5:13;16 (NKJV)

Father God,

Your Word tells us to pray in ALL circumstances. I thank You and give You praise because You meet me here every day and You listen to all my prayers. You are the one, true almighty God yet You come to me when I call. This morning, I come before You to specifically pray for those I know who need healing… (**Note**: *Communicate by name people who are in need*). I put them in Your hands and ask You to heal them and replace their fear with faith and peace. I also pray with gratitude for those things that bring me joy… (**Note**: *Communicate specific people, places, experiences, items, whatever comes to mind which bring you joy*). You are a good, good Father and I praise You for all these things. I would like to take time to also pray for… (**Note**: *Communicate specific requests that You have*). Again, I give You my deepest gratitude because I believe You hear my prayers and that You are always working. Thank You that I can come before Your throne, not in my own righteousness but in the righteousness that Jesus has covered me in. I pray all these things this morning in Jesus' name.

Song Suggestion: In Jesus Name (God of Possible) *by* Katy Nicole

May 22

Seek God

I love those who love me, and those who seek me early and diligently shall find me.

Proverbs 8:17 (Amp)

Father God,

Your love fills me with love and life. Thank You. I owe all to You. I seek You because You are all I need. You are the God who strengthens me and protects me. I seek You so that You will put Your truth in my mind, heart, and soul. I seek You so that I can hear You and have the courage and diligence to pursue You and obey You. I seek You so that You will guide me and hold me in Your loving arms every day. You give so many promises to those who seek You. In this moment, I am giving You love because You loved me first. I am seeking You diligently. I am grateful that You will be found. In Jesus' name I pray.

Song Suggestion: Come to the Well *by* Casting Crowns

May 23

Discouragement

Why are you cast down, O my inner self? And why should you moan over me and be disquieted within me? Hope in God and wait expectantly for Him, for I shall yet praise Him, my Help and my God.

Psalm 42:5 (Amp)

Father God,

Why do I repeatedly focus on all my problems? I think about and meditate on my disappointments, about things that discourage me. I allow these feelings to continually sink into my mind, and into my soul, where they poison my life. I forget that You are in charge, that You are my hope. You are waiting for me to ask for help, waiting for me to praise You even in times of trouble. I choose right now, right this minute, to change my thoughts and put my hope in You. I believe that You can help me rise above the disappointments and hurts in my life. I will wait for You to move. I will wait expectantly in Your Presence. I will praise You while I wait. I will seek to do Your will and if I am not sure of Your will, I will set out to help someone while I wait. Thank You for helping me turn my mind, my heart, and my attitude around so that I can live harmoniously with You and with everyone around me. I pray this prayer with praise to my God who is my helper in Jesus' name.

Song Suggestion: Oh My Soul *by* Casting Crowns

God's Love

I will be glad and rejoice in your unfailing love, for you have seen my troubles and you care about the anguish of my soul. You have not handed me over to my enemies but have set me in a safe place.

Psalm 31:7-8 (NLT)

Father God,

I love and am thankful that You see me in my mess. You see the chaos that I feel, and I create. You see all my reactions and You see the worst of me, yet You still love me with Your unconditional, steadfast, and faithful, deep love. You also continue to protect me - You pick me up and put me in a safe place. I am choosing to be joyful today, remembering how You love and take care of me. I am sitting quietly and letting Your love and care wash over me. I am choosing love, grace, joy, and gratitude today. In Jesus' name I pray.

Song Suggestion: How He Loves *by* David Crowder Band

May 25

Hope

Behold, the Lord's eye is upon those who fear Him [who revere and worship Him with awe], who wait for Him and hope in His mercy and loving-kindness,

Psalm 33:18 (Amp)

Father God,

Thank You that Your eye is on me because I wait and hope in Your mercy and Your loving-kindness. I have faith in You and put my hope in You to help me live now with a mindset and attitude guided by the Holy Spirit. I have faith and put my hope in You to fill me with Your spiritual gifts of love, peace, joy, goodness, kindness, patience, gentleness, and self-control. I have faith and put my hope in You so that I can come boldly to Your throne, not on my own, but with the grace and righteousness given to me by Jesus. I also have faith and a living hope that I will be with You forever. I sit quietly and think about all these things this morning. I am eternally grateful to You for this solid faith and hope. In Jesus' name I pray.

Song Suggestion: I Have This Hope *by* Tenth Avenue North

May 26

Perseverance

I don't mean to say that I have already achieved these things or that I have already reached perfection. But I press on to possess that perfection for which Christ Jesus first possessed me. No, dear brothers and sisters, I have not achieved it, but I focus on this one thing: Forgetting the past and looking forward to what lies ahead, I press on to reach the end of the race and receive the heavenly prize which God through Christ Jesus, is calling us.

Philippians 3:12-14 (NLT)

Father God,

Help me, help me, help me. My prayer today is simple and sincere. Help me to keep moving toward You. Empower me to increase my faith more and more. Guide me to trust in You not only for my salvation but for all that concerns me. Give me grace to do Your will. Help me to forgive others as You forgive me. Empower me to give grace and mercy to others as You give them to me. Guide me to encourage and bless others as You encourage and bless me. Help me to love others as You love me. Oh, empower me to press on, increasing my consistency. I put myself in Your hands as I trust You to help me. I love You, thank You and praise You for all that You do to keep me going in the right direction! I ask all these things in Jesus' name today.

Song Suggestion: Press On *by* Mandisa

May 27

I am a Child of God

That is, those who are the children of the flesh, these are not the children of God; but the children of the promise are counted as the seed.

Romans 9:8 (NKJV)

Father God,

I am so thankful to You for allowing me to become one of Your adopted children. I sit quietly this morning and think about the privilege I have been given to be able to say with confidence, "I am a child of God." I am loved as Your child. I am provided for. I am protected. I have been given all Your blessings: peace, hope, joy - even though I don't enjoy them enough. You are my Father. You will never leave me or forsake me. You love me unconditionally just as I am. I do not have to earn Your love. I do not have to perform perfectly. You know me and still love me and still call me Your child. For all these things I am grateful. I am in awe of Your unconditional love, and I praise You for being such a good, good Father. I pray with deep love for You in Jesus' name.

Song Suggestion: I Am Yours *by* NEEDTOBREATHE

Motivation

People may be pure in their own eyes, but the LORD examines their motives. Commit your actions to the LORD, and your plans will succeed.

Proverbs 16:2-3 (NLT)

Father God,

I want to please You. Help me to commit my thoughts, my words, and my actions to line up with Your ways and Your truths. Right now, I tend to do whatever I want - whatever suits me. I am not always thinking about You as I go about my daily routines. Help me to change that so that I am thinking about Your will and not my own in all my thoughts and decisions. Let 'Your will be done' be a way of life for me. Purify my motives so whatever I do is for the right reasons and not selfish ones. I am submitting my plans to You and then trusting that You will work things out for the best. I believe Your plans are pure, lovely, holy, and worthy. I praise You in this moment. In Jesus' name I pray.

Song Suggestion: My Heart is Yours *by* Kristian Stanfill

May 29

Pray for Others

For whatever is born of God overcomes the world. And this is the victory that has overcome the world - our faith. Who is he who overcomes the world, but he who believes that Jesus is the Son of God?

1 John 5:4-5 (NKJV)

Jesus,

I am amazed and filled with wonder, awe, and thanksgiving that You gave Your life for me and my family. You have overcome and because You have conquered and overcome, You have given me faith so that I can be a conqueror and an overcomer. I want the same for… (**Note**: *Communicate the names of people that You are praying for*). I am praying specifically for them this morning. I am asking You to do whatever it takes to open their eyes and hearts to You, Your truth, and Your love. I pray that (*names*) will come to have a firm, steadfast, deep faith in You and that they will also be conquerors and overcomers who live in Your victory every day. I believe You are a God who saves, and I am placing my family and friends in Your hands. Thank You God that You are the God Who saves. In Jesus' name I pray today.

Song Suggestion: Fight On My Knees *by* Evan Craft

May 30

I am... Salt of the Earth

"You are the salt of the earth; but if the salt loses its flavor, how shall it be seasoned? It is then good for nothing but to be thrown out and trampled underfoot by men.

Matthew 5:13 (NKJV)

Father God,

I know that I am so many things - I'm a mom/dad, son/daughter, friend, coworker, spouse. I have to say that I do not really think of myself as salt. Therefore, I am asking You to help me understand what being salt would look like in my everyday life. Help me understand what it takes to live a pure, holy life that 'flavors' the world around me. Help me to see opportunities to do good works and represent you well. Help me stay on Your path and not stray onto the wrong one. I need Your help to have courage to do what is right even if no one else does. I need Your help to step out of my comfort zone to lend a hand to someone in need. I need Your vision to see things the way You do. I ask You to help me be Your salt in this world every single day. I ask all these things in Jesus' name.

Song Suggestion: Do Something *by* Matthew West

May 31

I Will...

"You shall have no other gods before Me. You shall not make for yourself an idol, or any likeness of what is in heaven above or on the earth beneath, or in the water under the earth.

Exodus 20:3-4 (NASB)

Father God,

I will put You first in my life. I will spend time with You and learn about You, pray to You, and ask You to help me with all my decisions. I will put You first in my decisions for my family and myself. I will put You first in my relationships. I will count my blessings, and I will thank You for them. I will use my finances in a way to honor and serve You. I will be generous and compassionate. I want everything I do in my life to please You, Father. I ask You to help me see the areas where I do not put You first. Help me to make You the center of my life and not just an afterthought or someone I only think about on Sundays. I want to prioritize my life so that my life (my schedule, my activities, my entertainment choices, my free time choices) honor You. I sit quietly and think about putting You first in my life. I pray this prayer in Jesus' holy name.

Song Suggestion: I Surrender to You *by* Jeremy Camp

Holy, Sovereign God

Know, recognize and understand therefore this day and turn your [mind and] heart to it that the Lord is God in the heavens above and upon the earth beneath; there is no other.

Deuteronomy 4:39 (Amp)

Father God,

You are the Lord of heaven and earth. The one, true, holy God. There is no one like You. I believe You are here with me today. I live my life moving from task to task, getting things done and too often forgetting that You are waiting for me to invite You to guide me, teach me and bless me. Help me to know You and understand You. Plant Your ways into my heart and open my heart to You right now. I declare my faith in You. You are the one, true, holy, sovereign God who is in the heavens and upon the earth. There is no other God but You. I put all that I am into Your hands in this moment. I pray in Your Son, Jesus' name today.

Song Suggestion: God of Wonders *by* Third Day

Praise

Unto You, O my Strength, I will sing praises; for God is my Defense, my Fortress, and High Tower, the God Who shows me mercy and steadfast love.

Psalm 59:17 (Amp)

Father God,

This morning, I think about all that You are and all that You have done for me. I praise You for being my defense, my protection. I praise You because I can come to You as I am and You will be my refuge, my safe place. I praise You, for You show me loving kindness. I praise You and thank You. In this moment, I am meditating on Your love and Your loving ways toward me. I am amazed at how You show me love, even when I do not reciprocate. I will forever remember and be grateful to You for being my God who gives me strength and who shows me mercy and steadfast, never-ending love. I start this day with Your love in my heart and praise and profound gratitude for You on my lips and in my soul. I love to give You the praise You deserve. In Jesus' name I pray.

Song Suggestion: King of Kings *by* Hillsong Worship

June 3

Wisdom

[For my concern is] that their hearts may be braced (comforted, cheered, and encouraged) as they are knit together in love, that they may come to have all the abounding wealth and blessings of assured conviction of understanding, and that they may become progressively more intimately acquainted with and may know more definitely and accurately and thoroughly that mystic secret of God [which is] Christ (the Anointed One).

Colossians 2:2 (Amp)

Father God,

I still myself before You and think about the mysteries of You: You are the great "I am." You are three beings in one, Father, Son, and Holy Spirit, Your only Son was crucified by the ones You created, yet You gave forgiveness to all. Although You hold many mysteries I may not understand, I ask You to continue giving me the passion to deepen my relationship with You. Help me to make sure we have this time together so that I can talk to and just be with You each day. As I get closer to You, our relationship will grow as will my wisdom and knowledge of You. This is my deep desire. Thank You for drawing close to me. I pray in Jesus' name today.

Song Suggestion: Know You More *by* StoneBridge Worship

June 4

Forgiven

To Him all the prophets testify (bear witness) that everyone who believes in Him [who adheres to, trusts in, and relies on Him, giving himself up to Him] receives forgiveness of sins through His name.

Acts 10:43 (Amp)

Father God,

I want to take time this morning to reaffirm my faith once again in You and in Your plan for me. You have made a way for me through Jesus Christ, to come into a relationship with You - the living, holy God. I believe in You, and I believe in Jesus. I believe He is Your Son and the One who makes me new every day through His forgiveness. I rely on what Jesus did for me at the cross. I do not rely on myself. I cannot do enough good things. I cannot give enough money away; I cannot become holy enough or righteous enough on my own to earn forgiveness. You forgive me freely, so I thank You for being my living hope and giving me a loving Savior, Jesus who is my shepherd and my friend. I pray with deep gratitude for all You have done for me, in Jesus' name.

Song Suggestion: Forgiven and Loved *by* Jimmy Needham

Open Ears

Your ears will hear a word behind you, saying, "This is the way, walk in it," whenever you turn to the right or to the left.

Isaiah 30:21 (NASB)

Father God,

I sit before You in quietness this morning wondering how many times You have told me what to do while I ignored You and did what I wanted to do instead. Yet, You are quick to respond mercifully with forgiveness. You are the holy God who knows what is best. Your ways are true and will lead to blessings. Help me understand this truth. Anything that You want me to do (or not do) is to help me, not to hurt me or to take anything away.

Open my eyes, my ears, my mind, and heart to Your words and to Your Spirit. Give me the wisdom to follow Your ways. Thank You for Your guidance, Your unfailing patience, and love. I pray in Jesus' name today.

Song Suggestion: Speak To Me *by* Tommy Walker

Joy

I will greatly rejoice in the LORD, my soul shall be joyful in my God; For He has clothed me with the garments of salvation, He has covered me with the robe of righteousness, as a bridegroom decks himself with ornaments, and as a bride adorns herself with her jewels.

Isaiah 61:10 (NKJV)

God, My Father,

Thank You for showing me that I can choose to rejoice, I can choose joy. I thank You for saving me and adopting me into Your family. I thank You for my salvation! I thank You for covering me in righteousness through no effort on my part. I imagine, in this moment, You are covering me with a snow-white robe of righteousness. I meditate on Your goodness. I think about how I am Yours, I am holy, I am righteous, I am set apart. I choose to be joyful today because I am all these things. I pray this joyful, thankful prayer, in Jesus' name.

Song Suggestion: Your Love Defends Me *by* Matt Maher

Love God, Love Others

And become useful and helpful and kind to one another, tenderhearted (compassionate, understanding, loving-hearted), forgiving one another [readily and freely], as God in Christ forgave you.

Ephesians 4:32 (Amp)

Father God,

I meet with You this morning to thank You for being in my life. I praise You because You are all knowing, holy and perfect. You have forgiven me so I can forgive others. I invite You to come into my heart and mind more fully. With Your help, I can dedicate my life to being more like You. As You fill me with Your Spirit, I will be kinder to others. I will be more helpful. I will be more giving and more merciful. Help me to be useful to You in my little part of the world. I strive to be more compassionate, understanding, and tenderhearted. As I lean on You, I can freely choose to be a person who loves. May my actions be reflective of all the love You have showered on me. May Your will be done in my heart and in my life. In Jesus' name I pray.

Song Suggestion: Be The Moon *by* Chris Tomlin feat. Brett Young, Cassadee Pope

Names of God

Jehovah Nissi

In Hebrew, this name means, "The Lord is my banner."

So Joshua defeated Amalek and his people with the edge of the sword. Then the LORD said to Moses, "Write this for a memorial in the book and recount it in the hearing of Joshua, that I will utterly blot out the remembrance of Amalek from under heaven." And Moses built an altar and called its name, The-LORD-Is-My-Banner."

Exodus 17:13-15 (NKJV)

Father God,

Sometimes this world feels so out of control: so many responsibilities and burdens to bear; so many evil things happening: shootings, wars, terrorist acts. This morning, I run to You, Jehovah Nissi for You are my banner. You fought for Your people long ago and helped them to live a victorious life, and You will fight for me so that I can live in victory as well. Spiritually, I run into Your arms. I breathe in Your relaxed, refreshing, restoring pace. I forget all else except for You. You invite me to stay and live in Your Presence, under Your banner where I can find peace and rest. I can slow down and breathe you in. I am so thankful for our time together. I am so thankful that You are my banner, You are fighting for me, You do not leave me alone. I give thanks and praise that You are the God who was and who is, and You always will be. I give You thanks and praise because You are consistent and stable. I give thanks and praise to My Warrior Father God and Jesus Christ who gives me victory and peace. In Jesus' holy name I pray.

Song Suggestion: Banner *by* Brooke Ligertwood (Live)

June 9

Jesus

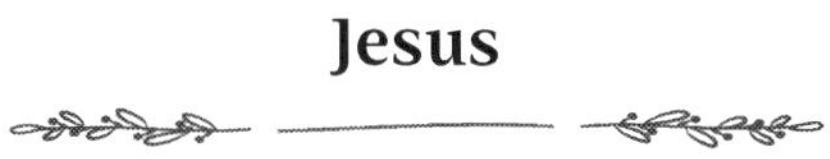

looking only at Jesus, the originator and perfecter of the faith, for the joy set before Him endured the cross, despising the shame, and has sat down at the right hand of the throne of God.

Hebrews 12:2 (NASB)

Jesus,

It amazes me how something that happened so long ago - specifically Your life and death 2000+ years ago - has changed me so profoundly. You gave Your love and poured it out on me. This love has touched me somehow. As I learn more of You and as I seek You increasingly, my awe and gratitude grow. I am so thankful that You continue to increase my faith. I am placing myself in Your hands so that You can continue as 'the author and finisher' of my faith. I am deciding that I will cooperate with You as You guide me. I surrender myself to You with love and gratitude. In Jesus' name I pray today.

Song Suggestion: Lead Me to the Cross *by* Brooke Ligertwood (with Martin Smith)

Eternity Minded

Nevertheless I am continually with You; You do hold my right hand. You will guide me with Your counsel, and afterward receive me to honor and glory.

Psalm 73:23-24 (Amp)

Father God,

You are with me now. I am with You- my mind, heart, and spirit. I am breathing the air You are giving me in this moment. I am slowing down and letting Your Presence settle over me and in me. You are holding my hand as I willfully hold Yours. I am filled with praise and gratitude for Your goodness. You are guiding me. Help me to be guidable and teachable. I have Your promise that You will take me into glory where I will continue to be with You, and I will be able to hold Your hand forever and we will be together for eternity. Oh, the joy and peace You give! Thank You, thank You. I praise You now and forever more. In Jesus' name I pray today.

Song Suggestion: I Will Rise *by* Chris Tomlin

June 11

Believing

But when the kindness and the love of God our Savior toward man appeared, not by works of righteousness which we have done, but according to His mercy He saved us, through the washing of regeneration and renewing of the Holy Spirit, whom He poured out on us abundantly through Jesus Christ our Savior.

Titus 3:4-6 (NKJV)

Father God,

I am pondering all the Good News that Your Word shares. You are so good, so loving and so kind. You have provided salvation for me - You have saved me. I thank You so much for Your gift to me. I do not need to pay any price. I do not need to do any work. But I stand before You now, thinking about all You have done for me and I want to repay You somehow, but how can I? I am here before You with empty hands, but my heart is full of love, gratitude, and a purpose to do my best each day to take this life You've given me and live it for You. I believe in You Father and I believe in Jesus. I thank You and love You. Hear my prayer that I pray today in Jesus' holy name.

Song Suggestion: Always *by* Chris Tomlin

Peace

Now may the Lord of peace Himself grant you His peace (the peace of His kingdom) at all times and in all ways [under all circumstances and conditions, whatever comes]. The Lord [be] with you all.

2 Thessalonians 3:16 (Amp)

Father God,

I believe You are the Lord of peace. I believe Your peace is unlike the world's peace which does not last. I am praying for Your peace over my life. I am asking You to continue to help me follow Your ways consistently, not only so I can please You but so that I can live a life that is peaceful and joyful so that others will see Christ living in me. In this moment, I am so joyful to be here with You. I love our time together and I know that this time with you connects us and secures Your peace in my life. Thank You for giving me Your peace in the good times when all is well with me. Thank You for giving me peace when things are not going well in my life, when there are troubles, anxieties, unsettling circumstances. Thank You for giving me peace in whatever comes. Thank You, Prince of Peace. In Jesus' name I pray.

Song Suggestion: Peace *by* Bethel Music feat. We the Kingdom

June 13

God's Will

So Jesus told them, "My message is not my own; it comes from God who sent me. Anyone who wants to do the will of God will know whether my teaching is from God or is merely my own. Those who speak for themselves want glory only for themselves, but a person who seeks to honor the one who sent him speaks truth, not lies.

John 7:16-18 (NLT)

Father God,

Today as I sit quietly with You, I would ask that You examine my heart. I want to do Your will, but I know that sometimes I do not. Help me to use my words and my actions to give You glory, not to gain attention or gain advantages for myself. Help me to recognize when I say or do things for selfish reasons. Guide me so that I act selflessly rather than selfishly. Guide me to speak Your truth, to myself and to others. Advise me so that my daily motivation pleases You, honors You. I am praying that Your will be done in my life. I am asking for a lot of help this morning to do Your will, Father. I am thankful that You hear my pleas, and I am filled with hopeful expectation that You will answer these prayers of mine. I pray in Jesus' name today.

Song Suggestion: My Offering *by* Journey Worship

Thoughts/Mindset

And set your minds and keep them set on what is above (the higher things), not on the things that are on the earth.

Colossians 3:2 (Amp)

Father God,

This morning, I come to You with a grateful heart for all You have given me in this world. I know that all good things come from You. When I read today's scripture, I realize that I am often focused on wanting 'earthly' things. I sometimes see what other people have and I feel I am missing out. But… Your Word tells me to set my mind and think about Your 'higher things.' Help me to create habits of praising You throughout the day. Help me to thank You intentionally for every little and big thing that I have in my life. Help me look for ways to be generous with my words, my attitude, my money, my "stuff,' my time. Guide me to be on the lookout for Your blessings given to me each day. Remind me that I am Yours and You love me just as I am. Help me take my mind off myself; I need to focus on You and all You have already given me. I pray that I will set my mind and keep it set on 'the higher things' - Your things. In Jesus' name I pray.

Song Suggestion: Just One of Those Days *by* 33Miles

June 15

The Presence of God

I have set the L*ORD always before me; because He is at my right hand I shall not be moved.*

Psalm 16:8 (NKJV)

Father God,

I thank You, praise You and glorify You for all You are doing in my life. You are my partner along with being so much more. You are helping and guiding me. I can turn to You all day, all night - every day, every night and You are with me. I do not have to live alone. I do not have to live according to my circumstances and my fickle feelings. I can trust You and depend on You because You have my back - even if there is trouble or things do not go the way I want or expect. I will walk step by step, day by day leaning on You, trusting You, conversing with You. You are an unstoppable God. You are unshakeable. You are always consistent and tranquil. I have set You before me. You are at my right hand, and I shall live in Your Presence. We will not be moved. I pray with deep gratitude for Your promises in Jesus' name today.

Song Suggestion: Call on Jesus *by* Bryan McCleery

June 16

Trust God

Behold, God is my salvation, I will trust and not be afraid; 'For YAH, the LORD, is my strength and song; He also has become my salvation.' "

Isaiah 12:2 (NKJV)

Father God,

This morning, I meditate on my faith in You. I believe You are my salvation. I believe You are good and You have saved me in both eternal life and this earthly life. I have faith that You are the one, mighty and holy Father in whom I can trust. I will trust You and not be afraid, worried, or anxious. I believe You are with me, You are strengthening me, and You will get me through all troubles to the other side where there is victory, joy, and peace. I will trust You without exception through all the ups and downs, I will remain stable because my faith is in You. I am choosing to go through all circumstances worshiping You, praising You, living in gratitude and living in Your love. In Jesus' trustworthy name I pray.

Song Suggestion: Trust In Jesus *by* Third Day

Forgiving

And Jesus prayed, Father, forgive them, for they know not what they do. And they divided His garments and distributed them by casting lots for them.

Luke 23:34 (Amp)

Father God,

You are a God who continually shows mercy, kindness, compassion, and forgiveness to me. After Jesus, who had done nothing wrong other than do Your will, was beaten, tortured, and put on a cross to die a slow and horrible death, He offered forgiveness to his torturers. Jesus, I am in awe of Your will in this moment. How could You do this, even as You were suffering? I am in awe of the love and mercy that You poured out to those around You who were so undeserving of it.

I am grateful for the love and mercy that You pour out on me even though I am undeserving of it. Thank You for the exceptional model of how to forgive others who have hurt You. Thank You for demonstrating forgiveness as an act of will. Help me to forgive others as You do. Help me to willfully choose forgiveness, regardless of how I feel. Help me to live my life, as You did, with forgiveness as a natural way to live. Help me to forgive as an act of worship and love to You. Thank You for Your peaceful ways. I ask all these things in Jesus' merciful name.

Song Suggestion: Thief *by* Third Day

My Words

Let your speech always be with grace, seasoned with salt, that you may know how you ought to answer each one.

Colossians 4:6 (NKJV)

Father God,

I take time to think about the scripture reading today and about how my speech should be gracious and pleasant. I am self-reflecting and asking myself, "Is this true for me at all times? Some of the time?" The truth is that this is an area that I need to improve. I need You to help me speak with Your grace and Your love no matter my mood or my feelings. Help me use my words to lift and bless others. Guide me to speak to myself and others with kindness and truth. Help me with my tone of voice so that what I say is optimistic and encouraging. I am learning more and more from Your Word that what I say and how I say it matters. I thank You for patiently teaching me and molding me into a person who has grace, mercy, and love for others. I really want to be more like You, and I want to represent You well. I love You and praise You today. In Jesus' name I pray.

Song Suggestion: Sing *by* Chris Tomlin feat. Russell Dickerson and Georgia Florida Line

June 19

Anxiety

Then the cares and anxieties of the world and distractions of the age, and the pleasure and delight and false glamour and deceitfulness of riches, and the craving and passionate desire for other things creep in and choke and suffocate the Word, and it becomes fruitless.

Mark 4:19 (Amp)

Father God,

You are enough. I am meditating on You this morning. It is so easy to get overwhelmed by my worries, my circumstances, my struggles. It is all too easy to get off Your path. If I allow it, I can be distracted from You by daily concerns. But today, I am running toward You (spiritually) with all my fears, worries and anxieties. I am trading them for You. I am putting You first in my life and I am trusting You with everything. Thank You for Your faithfulness. Thank You that You are guiding me even when I don't realize it. Thank You for Your Word which constantly reminds me that You are what I need; You are more than enough. I thank You that You are helping me stay close to You as I let go of all my fears. I praise You and honor You today. In Jesus' name I pray.

Song Suggestion: Be Alright *by* Danny Gokey, Evan Craft, and Redimi2

June 20

Thankful

Let us therefore, receiving a kingdom that is firm and stable and cannot be shaken, offer to God pleasing service and acceptable worship, with modesty and pious care and godly fear and awe.

Hebrews 12:28 (Amp)

Father God,

There are days where I must really dig deep and remember that there is a kingdom which is firm and stable and cannot be shaken. In this world I am living in right now, there are so many hurdles and complications that I face each day. Some are personal day-to-day struggles; some are the chaos and anarchy happening in families and communities throughout the world. The world seems like it is coming apart at the seams. But then I remember that You have authority over me. It is my purpose to focus on You and give gratitude to You that I do not belong to this world, but to You and Your Kingdom. I can lay all the chaos aside and I can worship You-for You are the holy, living, almighty God (My Father). I can live my life for You, living with hope, living in service, and living in a state of gratefulness. I can choose to be thankful every single day of my chaotic life for the blessing that I am a part of Your steadfast, holy, perfect kingdom! I pray this prayer in Your Son, Jesus' name today.

Song Suggestion: Give Thanks *by* Steffany Gretzinger feat. Melissa Hesler

Prayer

ALSO [Jesus] told them a parable to the effect that they ought always to pray and not to turn coward (faint, lose heart, and give up).

Luke 18:1 (Amp)

Father, Spirit, and Jesus,

You are the God of the universe and yet You want to be in close contact with me. You want me to ask for strength and You will help me not to lose heart or give up. You want me to share my joy and You will be joyful with me. I thank You that I do not have to be discouraged or discontent as You are the God of hope, the God of breakthroughs. I can talk to You all the time! I can bring You all my cares and burdens always. Right now, these are some of the things that have been on my mind… (**Note**: *Communicate to God whatever comes to Your mind*). I also want to share with You the joys that I am experiencing… (**Note**: *Communicate any good things happening in your life*). Thank You for the joys and blessings in my life. Thank You for helping me with my struggles. Thank You that You want me to share all these things with You. I am praising You because You are a God Who listens and Who cares for me. I pray all these things in Jesus' name today.

Song Suggestion: Keep Praying *by* Maverick City Music

June 22

Seek God

The Lord looked down from heaven upon the children of men to see if there were any who understood, dealt wisely, and sought after God, inquiring for and of Him and requiring Him [of vital necessity].

Psalm 14:2 (Amp)

Father God,

When You look down from heaven, I pray that You will see me. Although I cannot say I understand all of You and Your ways, I am working to increase my understanding. I am seeking after You because You are all I need. I believe You are giving me desperately needed wisdom and guidance. I believe You are with me, helping me along life's way. I believe that when I go down the wrong path You will pick me up and put me on the right path. I believe You are protecting me and watching over me. I believe in You and all Your goodness. I will continue to seek You as I need You each day. I bless You, thank You and praise You because I believe You see me. In Jesus' name I pray this morning.

Song Suggestion: Lord I Need You *by* Matt Maher

Discouragement

"Are not five sparrows sold for two copper coins? And not one of them is forgotten before God. "But the very hairs of your head are all numbered. Do not fear therefore; you are of more value than many sparrows.

Luke 12:6-7 (NKJV)

Father God,

I come to You this morning with a heart full of discouragement, disappointments that never seem to end. I bring them to You today... (**Note**: *Communicate to God what is on Your mind*). I am thankful for Jesus' words that remind me that I am important to You. I am valuable to You. I can remember that fact even though I have some battles in my life. I can still have faith that You are taking care of me. You are working all things out for good. You are sovereign and have a great plan for my life. I can let go of all bitterness and unforgiveness and I can put my problems in Your hands. I can let go of the idea that everything in life must be perfect for me to be content. I can let go of all my disappointments and my negative thoughts and feelings. Right now, in this moment, I am letting go, I am looking up and I am letting Your love fill me. I sit quietly with You now. As I start this new day, I am sending my love to You. I pray this prayer with deep gratitude in Jesus' name.

Song Suggestion: Sparrows and Lilies *by* Pat Barrett

God's Love

And this hope will not lead to disappointment. For we know how dearly God loves us, because he has given us the Holy Spirit to fill our hearts with his love. When we were utterly helpless, Christ came at just the right time and died for us sinners. Now, most people would not be willing to die for an upright person, though someone might perhaps be willing to die for a person who is especially good. But God showed his great love for us by sending Christ to die for us while we were still sinners.

Romans 5:5-8 (NLT)

Father God,

Thank You for sending Jesus to take our sins away and paving the way for us to be able to come to You and know You more thoroughly. Thank You, Jesus, for dying for me, knowing that when I came along, I would be faithless, prideful, and distant from You. Yet, You still went to the cross for me. I am in awe of your willingness to suffer and die for sinners - for people who disregard You, who ignore You, who are selfish. In this moment, I am remembering Yours and our Father's love for me. I accept this deep, free, unending love that You give. I will live in Your love every day. I will not forget or take for granted the love that You poured out on the cross. I will live with gratitude for my Father, for Jesus my Savior and for the Holy Spirit, my helper. In Jesus' name I pray today.

Song Suggestion: For the Love of God *by* Andrew Ripp

June 25

Hope

For I know the plans I have for you," says the L*ORD*. *"They are plans for good and not for disaster, to give you a future and a hope.*

Jeremiah 29:11 (NLT)

Father God,

Since the beginning of humankind, You have had plans for us. And I believe You have plans for me. Your plans are good. Your plans for my good will bring peace, joy, and continual hope. You are such a good, good Father and You want what is best for me. Help me follow Your plans. Thank You for opening doors of opportunity and for closing doors that would lead me away from the best path for me. Guide me to be obedient to Your ways so that I can be all You want me to be. I am so, so thankful that You, my holy and almighty Creator of all, would have a plan for my future. I thank You and praise You that You have plans for my well-being. I thank You and praise You for giving me hope. My hope is in You. I pray with deep gratitude in Jesus' name today.

Song Suggestion: I Know The Plans (I Have For You) *by* Lordsong

Perseverance

Here [comes in a call for] the steadfastness of the saints [the patience, the endurance of the people of God], those who [habitually] keep God's commandments and [their] faith in Jesus. Then I heard further [perceiving the distinct words of] a voice from heaven, saying, write this: Blessed (happy, to be envied) are the dead from now on who die in the Lord! Yes, blessed (happy, to be envied indeed) says the Spirit, [in] that they may rest from their labors, for their works (deeds) do follow (attend, accompany) them!

Revelation 14:12-13 (Amp)

Father God,

I thank You and praise You this morning for encouraging me to be persistently determined to follow You, follow Jesus and to remain faithful no matter what the outcome here on earth is. You are a God Who rewards! I am deciding today to continue following You, to continue learning about You and Your ways. I am going to live close to You and allow You into all areas of my life. I will have moments of weakness, I will fail, but I will get back up and start over again! Light that enduring, persistent fire in me, oh Lord! Help me shine for You consistently every day! In Jesus' name I pray.

Song Suggestion: Christ is Enough *by* Hillsong Worship

June 27

I am a Child of God

The people I formed for Myself, that they may set forth My praise [and they shall do it].

Isaiah 43:21 (Amp)

Father God,

Thank You for making me in Your image. You formed me and created me so I could live my life with You and for You. I love that You have adopted me into Your family. I love that I continue to grow closer to You as I experience more of You in my life. I want to be even closer to You. Every day as I pray to You and read scriptures from Your Word, I get to know You more and grow a little bit in my knowledge and insight of You. I realize that I can never praise You enough. I can never thank You enough. I am and forever will be Your child, formed and surrounded by Your love. I pray in deep gratitude for all these things in Jesus' holy name.

Song Suggestion: Spoken For *by* MercyMe

June 28

Motivation

Be alert and on your guard; stand firm in your faith (your conviction respecting man's relationship to God and divine things, keeping the trust and holy fervor born of faith and a part of it). Act like men and be courageous; grow in strength! Let everything you do be done in love (true love to God and man as inspired by God's love for us).

1 Corinthians 16:13-14 (Amp)

Father God,

I am so thankful for Your love. A love without end. The love of a creator and a father. A love of a divine man who chose to die for me, a love of a Savior. You love me just as I am. I am meditating in awe on Your deep, all-encompassing love this morning. I am praying that You will help me let Your profound, unconditional love impact me thoroughly and completely. Let Your love for me be the motivation to stand firm and to be courageous and strong in my faith. Let my thoughts, attitudes, and actions reflect Your love. Thank You for the opportunities that You give me every day. Thank You for motivating me to rise and shine for You daily. I send my love to You in this moment. In Jesus' holy name I pray.

Song Suggestion: Courageous *by* Casting Crowns

June 29

Pray for Others

"Moreover, as for me, far be it from me that I should sin against the LORD in ceasing to pray for you; but I will teach you the good and the right way.

1 Samuel 12:23 (NKJV)

Father God,

I come to You this morning so thankful that You are a Father who wants to hear from me. You listen and You care about all my requests and petitions. This morning, I am praying, not for myself, but for others. Specifically, I am praying for… (**Note**: *Communicate to God whoever is in Your heart to pray for*). I pray that they will hear from You in some way. I pray that You will help them in the way that is best. I pray that they will be surrounded by Your love and peace and that somehow, they will feel it and know that these feelings are from You. As for me, I pray that You will continue to guide me and teach me 'Your good and right way.' I pray with thanksgiving and praise all these things in Jesus' name.

Song Suggestion: Obey (Official Lyric Video) *by* Tiffany Hudson

June 30

I am… The Light of the World

"You are the light of the world. A city that is set on a hill cannot be hidden. "Nor do they light a lamp and put it under a basket, but on a lampstand, and it gives light to all who are in the house. "Let your light so shine before men, that they may see your good works and glorify your Father in heaven.

Matthew 5:14-16 (NKJV)

Jesus,

You are the light of the world. And yet You are telling me that I am the light of the world also. Empower me to shine Your light in this dark world I live in. Guide me to shine kindness where there is rudeness, disrespect, and cruelty. Guide me to shine calm and peace where there is chaos and agitation. Guide me to shine fruitful words and actions into the eyes of apathy and indifference. Wherever there is a need, help me to see it and meet it every day. Give me insight so that I can use Your words, use Your ideas, use Your wisdom to make a change and be the light that You created me to be. I am Your light in this world. Thank You for Your light shining on, in and through me. I pray in Jesus' holy name.

Song Suggestion: Learning to Be the Light *by* Newworldson

Holy, Sovereign God

Be still, and know that I am God; I will be exalted among the nations, I will be exalted in the earth!

Psalm 46:10 (NKJV)

Father God,

This morning, I am still and quiet as I sit and worship You in Your Presence. I am breathing in all that You are. Breathing in love, mercy, peace, kindness, goodness, and grace. As I breathe out, I send my deep gratitude, my praise, and all my love to You. I breathe in and out in this reverent, holy stillness and I am filled with tranquility and peace. I am so thankful for our time together. I am so thankful that You are God, my Father who is above us all. One day You will be exalted in all the earth. I am exalting You now. I am bowing before You and declaring that You are the one, holy, sovereign, true, pure God Almighty Who will reign forever. I thank You and praise You in this holy moment. I pray this prayer in Your Son, Jesus' name today.

Song Suggestion: Be Still *by* Newsboys

Praise

O Lord, You are my God; I will exalt You, I will praise Your name, for You have done wonderful things, even purposes planned of old [and fulfilled] in faithfulness and truth.

Isaiah 25:1 (Amp)

Father God,

This morning, I am focusing my thoughts and prayers on exalting and praising You. I believe that one of my purposes is to praise You. You are faithful and good. I praise You for You have done wonderful things. You are full of faithfulness and truth. I praise You now and trust that You are working on helping me fulfill the plans You have for me. I cannot wait to see how Your plans work out! In the meantime, I will focus on You. I will put You first in my life. I will get up every day with praise and gratitude for all that You are doing in my life. I praise You now with all my heart, mind, and soul. In Jesus' faithful name I pray.

Song Suggestion: All My Praise *by* Selah

July 3

Wisdom

Those who are wise will take all this to heart; they will see in our history the faithful love of the LORD.

Psalm 107:43 (NLT)

Father God,

Thank You for Your Word that helps me see all the good things You do. You are my provider, my protector, my Savior, my healer, my friend. I am concentrating on all You have given. I am thinking about all You have done. I remember all You have done for our country and how You have stepped in and helped us to be victorious and strong. I stop and focus on Your lovingkindness. I thank You and praise You. This is where wisdom starts - with You. Empower me with Your wisdom so that I know how to build my life around You, so I can live in obedience to You. As I center my life around You, I ask that my strength, courage, discernment and patience would grow. I pray with deep appreciation for Your guidance in Jesus' name.

Song Suggestion: Build my Life *by* Pat Barrett

July 4

Forgiveness

O Lord, to us belong confusion and shame of face - to our kings, to our princes, and to our fathers- because we have sinned against You. To the Lord our God belong mercy and loving-kindness and forgiveness, for we have rebelled against Him;

Daniel 9:8-9 (Amp)

Father God,

I come before You this morning with a heart and mind full of thanksgiving to You. I am thankful for Your loving-kindness, thankful for Your mercy and thankful for Your forgiveness. I have fostered and acted upon anger. I have lied, I have been unkind, I have been selfish, I have been greedy. I have not treated others the way I would like to be treated. And yet, You still meet me here with open arms, with love, mercy, and with forgiveness. Oh, how good You are! Oh, how I praise You for all these blessings that You give me. Help me to be aware of my sins so that I can change and live a life most pleasing to You. Help me today and every day.

I also pray for our country today. I pray that we all recognize that we need You and Your ways. I pray that we seek You more, follow You more and do Your will. I pray that our leaders turn to You for Your wisdom and Your help. I pray all these things in Jesus' name.

Song Suggestion: That's How You Forgive *by* Shane and Shane

Open Ears

So we must listen very carefully to the truth we have heard, or we may drift away from it.

Hebrews 2:1 (NLT)

Father God,

I am happy to start my day with You. I am so thankful for our time together. I am thankful for the truth that I am learning from You through the scriptures. I am learning to be mindful that I need to be listening consistently to You and what You say. Please open my ears to listen intently so that I may apply Your truth to my life. Help me to understand what is best for me to do. When I am not sitting here quietly with You but am out living my life, guide me so that I am actively walking in Your ways and in Your truth. I ask You to bring me closer to You; don't let me drift away from You. Empower me to remain firm and strong. I thank You and praise You for You are my teacher and my guide. I thank You and praise You because You are my anchor. In Jesus' holy name I pray.

Song Suggestion: Drifter *by* Decemberadio

Joy

Honor and majesty are [found] in His presence; strength and joy are [found] in His sanctuary.

1 Chronicles 16:27 (Amp)

Father God,

I take time this morning to remember how holy, how high above me You are. I bow down before You, remembering that You are surrounded by majesty. In You, I find strength. In You, I find joy. In You, I find love. I realize that I can only find joy and strength in You. I need You, Lord. I sit in Your Presence this morning and I soak up Your joy. As I move into the busyness of the day, I pray that You will remind me to take time to lean into You, into Your strength and into Your joy throughout all my day. Thank You for these blessings. This is the abundant life that I can only get through You. In Jesus' name I pray.

Song Suggestion: House of the Lord *by* Phil Wickham

July 7

Love God/Love Others

I am giving you a new commandment, that you love one another; just as I have loved you, that you also love one another. By this all people will know that you are My disciples: if you have love for one another."

John 13:34-35 (NASB)

Father God,

Thank You for giving us the gift of Jesus Who showed the depth of Your love. Jesus, You command us to love others. Help me to put this into practice as You did. I need Your guidance. I need Your vision and wisdom so I can represent You as I go out into the world. I confess that I am often selfish and unaware of how I can show love in my everyday life. I ask You to show me Your ways. Fill me with Your love so that it flows out to all of those around me. I am deciding right now, in this moment, that I will be bold and courageous. I will be generous, kind, and compassionate to my family and to all people whom I encounter. I will do my best to obey Your commandment to love. I pray in Jesus' name today.

Song Suggestion: Brother *by* NEEDTOBREATHE

Names of God

Jehovah Raah

Translated from Hebrew, Jehovah Raah means The Lord is my shepherd. It encompasses the life-giving care and tenderness that a shepherd gives his flock.

The Lord is my Shepherd; I shall not want.

Psalm 23:1 (NKJV)

Father God,

Thank You for being my shepherd. Thank You for watching over me, for shielding me, for guiding me, for meeting all my needs. I believe You are leading me. Continue to guide me and give me the courage and strength to follow You. And when I go my own way, I thank You for being patient with me. Thank You for coming to get me, for picking me up and putting me on the right path. Thank You for pursuing me. I praise You and thank You for being my Lord and my Shepherd. I pray in Jesus' name today.

Song Suggestion: My Shepherd (Psalm 23) *by* Aaron Shust

Jesus

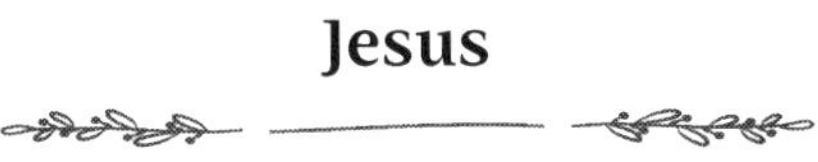

Jesus spoke to the people once more and said, "I am the light of the world. If you follow me, you won't have to walk in darkness, because you will have the light that leads to life."

John 8:12 (NLT)

Jesus,

This morning, I close my eyes and I declare that You are who You say You are. You are the light of the world. I lean toward Your light as I envision Your light streaming down upon me. Fill me with Your light, help me get rid of any sin and darkness in my life. I want to shine for You every day. I want Your light to shine upon me and touch everyone I meet. I welcome Your goodness and Your light. I will do my best to follow You daily. I thank You and praise You for the life You are leading me into. I pray in Your good and holy name, Jesus.

Song Suggestion: Light of the World *by* We the Kingdom

Eternity

"Let not your heart be troubled; you believe in God, believe also in Me. "In my Father's house are many mansions; if it were not so, I would have told you. I go to prepare a place for you. "And if I go and prepare a place for you, I will come again and receive you to Myself; that where I am, there you may be also.

John 14:1-3 (NKJV)

Jesus,

You have made such wonderful promises. You tell me that I have a special place that You are preparing for me in my future home! You have promised to come back and take me to Yourself, so I can be with You forever, for eternity! I believe You, Jesus. I believe You came to this earth, You died on the cross, so I could be forgiven. You rose again, and You are coming back to take us home. So, I will worship You and follow You while I wait. Help me to let Your kingdom come, and to do Your will while I wait. I thank You for Your assurances. With gratitude and praise, I pray this prayer in Your eternal name.

Song Suggestion: Spirit in the Sky *by* DC Talk

July 11

Believing

God saved you by his grace when you believed. And you can't take credit for this; it is a gift from God. Salvation is not a reward for the good things we have done, so one of us can boast about it.

Ephesians 2:8-9 (NLT)

Father God,

Thank You for Your grace, Your mercy, Your kindness. Thank You for making a way for me, for providing a Savior for me, for giving me a life with You now and into eternity. I will never be good enough, holy enough, perfect enough. But because I believe in Your perfect and holy Son Jesus, You say I am enough. Because I believe in the crucifixion of Jesus, You accept me into Your family. Because I believe in the resurrection of Jesus, I am Yours forever. I am always thankful for You, Jesus. I worship and serve You, not to earn my way into heaven but to show You my heart of gratitude and love. Thank You Father for saving me and giving me faith. I pray in Jesus' saving name.

Song Suggestion: This I Believe (Creed) *by* Hillsong Worship

July 12

Peace

And let the peace of God rule in your hearts, to which also you were called in one body; and be thankful.

Colossians 3:15 (NKJV)

Jesus,

I need You. I need more of Your peace every day. Many times throughout my days I am unsettled, chaotic, stressed out, agitated. You have called me to be different - to live in peace and in a state of gratitude. Please help me remember to 'let the peace of God rule in my heart.' Guide me in Your peaceful ways. Remind me that Your peace is within me, that I can stop and quiet myself by leaning into You anytime. I am so thankful that I have You to learn from and to depend on. You are my refuge who I can always run to.

Thank You Jesus, I thank You always. I pray in Jesus' peaceful name today.

Song Suggestion: It Is Well *by* Bethel Music

July 13

God's Will

For it is God's will and intention that by doing right [your good and honest lives] should silence (muzzle, gag) the ignorant charges and ill informed criticisms of foolish persons. [Live] as free people, [yet] without employing your freedom as a pretext for wickedness; but [live at all times] as servants of God.

1 Peter 2:15-16 (Amp)

Father God,

I am so thankful for the gift of Your freedom! I do not need to live my life to please others - I am free from that- I only want to please You. I am free to do "good and right" things as best as I know how. And when I make mistakes, I can come to You and ask for mercy, instruction and help and You forgive me, just like that! I am free from guilt and condemnation. I am learning that I am free to lean on You. I can accept Your joy and peace. I am free to be Your light every day. And these things are Your will for me! I am blessed all because of You. I honor and bless You in this moment with a heart filled with love and gratitude. I pray this prayer in Jesus' name this morning.

Song Suggestion: Your Will Be Done *by* CityAlight

Thoughts/Mindset

For truly, let not such a person imagine that he will receive anything [he asks for] from the Lord, [For being as he is] a man of two minds (hesitating, dubious, irresolute), [he is] unstable and unreliable and uncertain about everything [he thinks, feels, decides].

James 1:7-8 (Amp)

Father God,

In this scripture, James gets right to his point: As Your child I need a stable, consistent, reliable faith and mindset. I trust that You are helping me, but You know my work is not finished. Thank You for Your patience with me. Thank You for helping me become more consistent in my thoughts, attitudes, and mindset. Counsel me not to be frustrated with myself but to be confident in Your leadership and guidance. Even though I am not perfect, I am moving in the right direction! I am depending on You - my guide, counselor, teacher. I will do my part and live with the intention of keeping my mind and my eyes on You. Father, You are perfect. You are mighty. You are holy. You are to be praised and lifted high. I lift You high in my life today. In Jesus' name I pray.

Song Suggestion: Reason to Praise *by* Cory Asbury feat Naomi Raine

The Presence of God

And the Lord said, My Presence shall go with you, and I will give you rest. And Moses said to the Lord, If Your Presence does not go with me, do not carry us up from here!

Exodus 33:14-15 (Amp)

Father God,

Thank You for the picture You have given us of Moses who does not want to do anything without Your Presence. Thank You that You are a God who invites us into Your Presence. You invite **me**, personally, into Your Presence. You are a God who wants to be with me, and You will give me rest. This morning, I close my eyes and enter Your Presence with praise and thanksgiving. I praise You for all You have done, are doing, and will do. I thank You for Your goodness, Your plans for peace, for rest, for ALL that You are. I sit quietly and let Your tranquility and holiness saturate my heart and soul. I let Your Spirit renew me completely. I start my day thoroughly in awe of You. Help me to stay in Your Presence as I enter the busyness of this day. Give me the mindset of Moses: If your Presence does not go with me, I do not want to go! I pray in Jesus' name today.

Song Suggestion: Pour Your Spirit Out *by* Thrive Worship

Trust God

The LORD is my strength and my shield; my heart trusted in Him, and I am helped; Therefore my heart greatly rejoices, and with my song I will praise Him.

Psalm 28:7 (NKJV)

Father God,

As I turn to You this morning and run to You, I believe You are helping me in the trials in my life. I am deciding that I will trust in You with everything. (**Note**: *Communicate to God in what areas/situations that You are specifically trusting God.*) I admit there are times when I live on my own, do things my own way before remembering that I can turn to You, my help, my strength, my shield. You will guide me on the best path, Your path, as I yield to You. Help me remember to quiet myself so that I can stay in close contact with You. As I pray right now, I am directing my heart and mind to put my faith and my trust completely in You. I am receiving (by faith) Your joy and rest. I am praising You because You are so faithful. I am thanking You because I can count on You to help and guide me. I am thanking You because You are so, so good. My heart shall sing to You all day long. In Jesus' name I pray.

Song Suggestion: Faithful Now *by* Vertical Worship

Forgiving

Blessed (happy, to be envied, and spiritually prosperous - with life-joy and satisfaction in God's favor and salvation, regardless of their outward conditions) are the merciful, for they shall obtain mercy!

Matthew 5:7 (Amp)

Father God,

You are the author of mercy. You sent Your only Son to show me forgiveness when You sacrificed Jesus on the cross to pay the price for my sins. Jesus says that I am blessed when I am merciful to others. Oh, how I long to be consistently merciful. I ask You to open my eyes in moments when I have opportunities to show mercy. Let me see clearly so I can choose forgiveness. I put my attitude and my thoughts in Your hands as I seek this. Change me from the inside out. Help me to start right now. If there is someone that I need to forgive, I am deciding right now that I will forgive them. (**Note**: *Communicate to God anyone who comes to mind.*) I thank You for the opportunity to be blessed rather than to be bitter and angry. I thank You for the joy and satisfaction that You give me when I am merciful. I thank You for all Your blessings. In Jesus' merciful name I pray today.

Song Suggestion: Live Like You Were Dying *by* Tim McGraw

Words

The mouth of the righteous is a well of life, but violence covers the mouth of the wicked.

Proverbs 10:11 (NKJV)

Father God,

I am praying today about my big mouth! I realize that I fall short of Your perfection. However, I can sense Your hand reaching out to me, dusting me off and sending me out to try again. Today is a new day. Your mercies and Your help are new every morning.

Thank You that I can start fresh today. I make a commitment to You, in this moment, that with Your help, I will do my best to be a 'well of life' and a source of blessing with my words. I will not complain but will give thanks. I will speak excellent and right things. I will lean on Your Holy Spirit to help me say the right things at the right time. I will lean on Your Holy Spirit to keep my mouth closed when needed. Jesus has made me righteous. In His name, I begin today to do my best to speak righteously. Thank You for Your instruction. Thank You for all Your blessings and the life which You have given me. I pray in Jesus' name.

Song Suggestion: Sing a Song *by* 3rd Day

Anxiety

He makes me to lie down in green pastures; He leads me beside the still waters. He restores my soul; He leads me in the paths of righteousness for His name's sake. Yea, though I walk through the valley of the shadow of death, I will fear no evil; for You are with me; Your rod and Your staff, they comfort me. You prepare a table before me in the presence of my enemies; You anoint my head with oil; my cup runs over. Surely goodness and mercy shall follow me all the days of my life; and I will dwell in the house of the LORD Forever.

Psalm 23:2-6 (NKJV)

Father God,

I sit quietly and pray this psalm over again. I feel Your Presence. You are truly my Shepherd, You give me all that I need. When I slow down, quiet myself and lean into You, I know that You are refreshing and restoring me. No matter what is going on, no matter what the circumstances, You are with me, surrounding me, comforting me. May Your goodness and mercy fill my soul and overcome all my anxieties. It is in Your Presence that I am peaceful. Help me to live in Your Presence. Help me to tap into this peace, the peace that You provide, whenever I am anxious. Guide me to replace my anxious thoughts with the thoughts: "You are all I need," "You are with me," "Goodness and mercy are following me." Thank You for ALL You do. In Jesus' peaceful name I pray today.

Song Suggestion: Psalm 23 *by* Phil Wickham feat. Tiffany Hudson

Thankful

Enter into His gates with thanksgiving and a thank offering and into His courts with praise! Be thankful and say so to Him, bless and affectionately praise His name! For the Lord is good; His mercy and loving-kindness are everlasting, His faithfulness and truth endure to all generations.

Psalm 100:4-5 (Amp)

Father God,

I am so glad to be starting this new day with You. You are so good, full of mercy and loving kindness that does not end. I am thanking You and praising You for all You are. You have given me countless blessings. I can start with the very breath You breathe into me each day. I thank You for my parents, my family and all the positive people You have surrounded me with since I was young. Yes, I have hardships, struggles and pain but You are faithful to me. You always help me overcome and You will continue to. I thank You for all the blessings You have sent and continue to send. I look up to You with a grateful heart, soul, and mind. I pray with deep, deep gratitude today in Jesus' name.

Song Suggestion: Been So Good *by* Elevation Worship feat. Tiffany Hudson

Prayer

And this is the confidence (the assurance, the privilege of boldness) which we have in Him: [we are sure] that if we ask anything (make any request) according to His will (in agreement with His own plan). He listens to and hears us.

1 John 5:14 (Amp)

Father God,

You are a God, a Father, who cares about me. You hear me when I come to You. You hear my big prayers in our quiet times like this. But You also hear my little prayers as I go through the day. I am blessed because I have faith and confidence that You will draw close to me as I send my prayers to You. I am so amazed that You, the holy, almighty Creator of all, that You who sits on the throne of heaven with angels and saints praising You, that You know me, and listen to me. How amazing, wonderful You are. I close my eyes and send my worship, my praise to You now. I am so, so thankful that You listen and hear me. It is in Jesus' holy name I pray today.

Song Suggestion: God Help Me *by* Unspoken

July 22

Seek God

But if from there you will seek (inquire for and require as necessity) the Lord your God, you will find Him if you [truly] seek Him with all your heart [and mind] and soul and life.

Deuteronomy 4:29 (Amp)

Father God,

Help me put aside all that is on my mind this morning so that I can focus all my attention on You. I thank You that as we meet this morning, You are with me. I am seeking You this morning with all my heart and all my soul. I know that as I spend time with You, You are making my paths straight. You are renewing my mind and filling me with all good things. I will take Your goodness with me everywhere I go. I ask that You continue to light my way so that I am walking on Your paths, in Your light. I am asking You to put Your thoughts in my mind as You help me erase thoughts that are not from You. I believe You are in me and I am in You. With deep gratitude and awe, I pray this prayer in Jesus' name.

Song Suggestion: Calling for a Flood *by* John Waller

July 23

Discouragement

Hear, O Lord, have mercy and be gracious to me! O Lord, be my helper! You have turned my mourning into dancing for me; You have put off my sackcloth and girded me with gladness,

Psalm 30:10-11 (Amp)

Father God,

You are a good, good Father. You have given to me and blessed me with so much. Even so, If I am to be honest, I would like to be in total control of my life and my loved ones.

As You know, this is not possible, and this leads to feelings of discontentment, discouragement, and disappointment. I can be honest with You because You care about all of me. So, I bring You my disappointment and discouragement today and I ask you to be gracious to me, show favor to me, be my helper. I believe You are working things out. I believe You work all things out for good. I believe that You will turn my feelings of discouragement to joy as I take my focus off all my problems and put my focus on You. I will praise You now and later. I will praise You while I am waiting. I will give thanks to You forever. I pray in Jesus' name.

Song Suggestion: Shelter *by* Pat Barrett

God's Love

The LORD has appeared of old to me, saying: "Yes, I have loved you with an everlasting love; Therefore with lovingkindness I have drawn you.

Jeremiah 31:3 (NKJV)

Father God,

From the beginning of time, You have consistently shown lovingkindness. I am so grateful for Your everlasting love. I sit quietly this morning letting this unconditional, never ending love soak into my entire being. It does not matter what I have done, or not done. It does not matter what I have said, or not said. It does not matter what I look like, what my numbers are (weight and age). It does not matter how far I have roamed away from You. Your love for me is steadfast. I run to You now and open myself to Your immense love. I accept Your love. I accept Your lovingkindness. I invite You into every part of my life. Your love makes me want to please You. I send my deep gratitude and praise to You for this love that changes me. I send You my love and all that I am in this moment. In Jesus' holy name I pray.

Song Suggestion: Perfectly Loved *by* Rachel Lampa

July 25

Hope

Let us hold tightly without wavering to the hope we affirm, for God can be trusted to keep his promise.

Hebrews 10:23 (NLT)

Father God,

You give me hope. I ask You to help me seize it, to hold onto it without forgetting and letting it go. I believe that my faith and hope in You will bring me life and help me get through any tough times that come. I believe You are faithful. You are with me, and You are strengthening me and guiding me along. I sit silently with You this morning, grateful for the beautiful hope that I have in You. I do not know where I would be without You giving me hope, strength, courage, determination, faith, and love. I quiet myself as I declare that You are my hope, now and forever. I intentionally hold tightly to the hope that You give me. You are faithful and trustworthy to keep Your promises. I pray with gratitude for all that You give me in Jesus' name.

Song Suggestion: All My Hope *by* David Crowder

Perseverance

For if we are faithful to the end, trusting God just as firmly as when we first believed, we will share in all that belongs to Christ.

Hebrews 3:14 (NLT)

Father God,

I am here with You this morning because I believe in You. I want to increase my faith in You to a greater degree. I want to get closer to You every day. It is too easy to get off track, to slide into a bad attitude: to allow bitterness, anger, or regret to overtake me. In the world I live in, maintaining excellence, integrity, persistent kindness, and compassion in the face of constant adversity is turning out to be a lot more difficult than I could have imagined. But… I am setting my mind on You, on purpose every day. I am deciding to stand strong in You. I will be persistent in following You as best I can. Help me maintain this mindset. Help me persevere and hold firm to You Father, Jesus, and Holy Spirit. I pray this prayer with praise in Jesus' name.

Song Suggestion: I Won't Give Up (Christian Worship Version) *by* Jason Mraz

July 27

I am a Child of God

For you are all children of God through faith in Christ Jesus. And all who have been united with Christ in baptism have put on Christ, like putting on new clothes. There is no longer Jew or Gentile, slave or free, male and female. For you are all one in Christ Jesus. And now that you belong to Christ, you are the true children of Abraham. You are his heirs, and God's promise to Abraham belongs to you.

Galatians 3:26-29 (NLT)

Father God,

I am placing my body, spirit, soul in Your hands right now. I am so grateful that You have been and continue to renew me, to transform me. You have given me a firm faith. You have set me apart because I am Your child. You make me righteous and holy. I cannot do this myself. I need You Father, Spirit, and Jesus. Continue to guide me so I can participate in all the good plans that You have for me as Your child. And as I sit with You this morning and breathe in Your free gifts of love and peace, I am filled with love, gratitude, and praise for You, my living Father and my Savior, Jesus. I pray as Your heir, as Your son/daughter in Jesus' name today.

Song Suggestion: Children of God *by* Third Day

Motivation

For we speak as messengers approved by God to be entrusted with the Good News. Our purpose is to please God, not people. He alone examines the motives of our hearts.

1 Thessalonians 2:4 (NLT)

Father God,

Sometimes I find it hard to believe that You approved of me and that You could love me so deeply and unconditionally when I am so far from what I think You want from me.

Your Word tells me over and over that I am covered. I am forgiven. I am loved. I am approved. I set my purpose in my heart to please You more. I ask the Holy Spirit to help me to remain internally, spiritually motivated to put You first in my life. You see the true motivation of my heart. You know when I am doing 'good things' not for You, but for recognition or to get something. Help me see my own motivations for what they truly are. Help me to please You first. You deserve to be first in my life. You deserve all my praise and gratitude. I pray this prayer in Jesus' name.

Song Suggestion: Legacy *by* Nichole Nordeman

Pray for Others

But as for you, when you pray, go into your inner room, close your door, and pray to Your Father who is in secret; and your Father who sees what is done in secret will reward you.

Matthew 6:6 (NASB)

Father God,

Thank You for not only seeing me pray but for hearing all my prayers. I am full of gratitude that You want to hear me, You want me to stay in communication with You. So, I sit here with You, in this moment, following Your directive to pray in private. I am so grateful because I have come to love our quiet time together. I love knowing that You are here with me, wrapping me in Your love, peace, and hope. You are intently listening to my words, my thoughts and what is in my heart. You know all my deepest needs and wants, yet You want me to share them. This morning, I am thinking about other people in my life who need You in their lives as well. Specifically, I am thinking about… (**Note**: *Communicate to God your prayers for other people in your life who have healing needs, spiritual needs, financial needs, etc.*). I am lifting them up to You, Lord. Let Your will be done in their lives and in mine as well. I pray all these prayers in Jesus' name today.

Song Suggestion: We Pray *by* Barlow Girl

July 30

I am… Complete

Beware lest anyone cheat you through philosophy and empty deceit, according to the tradition of men, according to the basic principles of the world, and not according to Christ. For in Him dwells all the fullness of the Godhead bodily; and you are complete in Him, who is the head of all principality and power.

Colossians 2:8-10 (NKJV)

Father, Spirit, Jesus,

Today I meditate on how You make me complete. Although You say I am complete, I believe I am only complete in You. Without You, I can do nothing, and I am nothing. It is Your miracle working wonder that creates in me lasting change. So, as I sit in Your Presence and accept the promise that I am complete in You, I let Your completeness and Your version of who I am surround me and fill me while I am soaking it in. I am amazed by how You settle me and give me rest and tranquility. As I live each day, I will try my best to remember that You make me complete. You fill in my gaps. Your strength will override my weakness. I am enough. I am safe with You. I pray in gratitude and love in Jesus' holy name.

Song Suggestion: Made Whole *by* CRC Music

I Will...

Therefore encourage (admonish, exhort) one another and edify (strengthen and build up) one another, just as you are doing.

1 Thessalonians 5:11 (Amp)

Father God,

There is a lot of discouragement, disillusionment, despondency, and hopelessness in the world that we live in. I am so grateful that You give me a way out of all of that. You give me hope! You give me faith that all things will work out for good! You give me a choice to live differently than the world in all its negativity. You give me life and life to the fullest. I will live Your way. I will be an encourager. I will use my words to encourage others who have lost hope, who have lost their way, who are discouraged. I know that it is You who changes people, not me or my words. However, I will continue to shower Your love and Your encouragement on those around me. I will continue to strengthen and build up other people. I will pray that You will use my encouraging words to help others see Your light, Your truth, Your ways. I ask You to give me Your words. I ask You to open my eyes to the opportunities that You provide. I ask You to keep me encouraged so that I will encourage all those around me. In Jesus' holy name I pray this prayer.

Song Suggestion: Write Your Story *by* Francesa Battistelli

Holy Sovereign God

[And Ezra said], You are the Lord, You alone; You have made heaven, the heaven of heavens, with all their host, the earth, and all that is on it, the seas and all that is in them; and You preserve them all, and the hosts of heaven worship You.

Nehemiah 9:6 (Amp)

Father God,

I thank You today for Your amazing works. I think about all that You have created: thousands of mammals, tens of thousands of different trees and thousands of different kinds of fish. Wow! As I think about all Your creation, I see that You are utterly amazing. I am in awe of Your creative power, and I join in with the angels in bowing down before You in worship. I declare, with the prophet Ezra from long ago, You alone are the Lord. I thank You for life all around me and the abundant spiritual life You have given me. I pour out praise and gratitude to You, the Lord of ALL. I pray in Jesus' name today.

Song Suggestion: Echo Holy *by* Red Rocks Worship

Praise

Amen! (So be it!) they cried, Blessing and glory and majesty and splendor and wisdom and thanks and honor and power and might [be ascribed] to our God to the ages and ages (forever and ever, throughout the eternities of the eternities)! Amen! (So be it)

Revelation 7:12 (Amp)

Father God,

This moment in heaven angels and saints are praising You. I lift my voice with theirs and say glory to You, my Father. You are perfect in every way. I ask You, in this time we share together, to open my eyes and my mind to comprehend Your power, Your majesty. I stop everything this morning to focus on You - the God Who deserves glory, thanksgiving, and honor. You are the God who created me and all that I love and all that I have. You are the God who is all powerful yet still loves me and listens to me. Right now, in this moment, I send You all my heart filled with love and praise and profound gratitude. I will love You and praise You for all that You are forever. I join the angels in praise and worship. In Jesus' name I pray today.

Song Suggestion: Exalted (Yahweh) *by* Chris Tomlin

Wisdom

Fear of the LORD is the foundation of true knowledge, but fools despise wisdom and discipline.

Proverbs 1:7 (NLT)

Father God,

Help me to understand Your eminence, Your holiness, Your majesty. Help me to welcome Your wisdom, Your teaching, Your instruction and even Your correction. Help me to not only listen to what You say but to understand and then actually do what You want me to do. Guide me so that my faith helps me make the right choices with what I think, say, and do. I am so thankful that You will continue to give me wisdom as I seek You. I am so thankful that You are a patient God who will lead me step by step. I will take each step with You today at my side. I pray for all these things with deep gratitude and praise in Jesus' name.

Song Suggestion: Wisdom Song *by* Laura Woodley Osman

August 4

Forgiven

If we say that we have no sin, we deceive ourselves, and the truth is not in us. If we confess our sins, He is faithful and just to forgive us our sins and to cleanse us from all unrighteousness.

1 John 1:8-9 (NKJV)

Father God,

When I read today's scripture, I must admit and tell You that I am broken and sinful. I often choose to ignore this fact and think, "I am really not that bad - there are so many other people who do worse things." While this may be true, You are directing me to look at myself and realize that I do break Your commandments on a regular basis. Therefore, I take time this morning to think about and confess my sins to You. (**Note**: *Communicate to God any sins that come to mind.*) I am sorry for my errors and others that I may not even be aware of. Thank You that I am loved and forgiven. I thank You and praise You because Your love covers me and my faults. It is Your cleansing and forgiveness that frees me. So, today I will live for You, filled with Your love and mercy - ready to give others this love and mercy that flows through me. I pray this prayer in Jesus' holy name.

Song Suggestion: How Can It Be *by* Lauren Daigle

Open Ears

And I have other sheep [beside these] that are not of this fold. I must bring and impel those also; and they will listen to My voice and heed My call, and so there will be [they will become] one flock under one Shepherd.

John 10:16 (Amp)

Father God and Jesus,

I believe You are the Shepherd. I am a sheep. I am one who belongs to You. I want to hear Your voice and attend to You. I want to follow where You lead me. Open my ears so that I can hear You. With all the noise, the busyness, and the voices in this world, help me to quiet myself often and come back to You. Help me to hear You when I am making big decisions but also the little day to day decisions too. I am quieting myself now and every day when we meet so that I may listen to Your voice. I am thanking You for adopting me as one of Your "sheep." I am thankful to be in Your flock. I am trusting You as my leader, as my shepherd. I pray with deep gratitude and praise in Jesus' name.

Song Suggestion: God of Peace *by* Nikki Moltz, Josh Barnett

Joy

You have made known to me the ways of life; You will enrapture me [diffusing my soul with joy] with and in Your presence.

Acts 2:28 (Amp)

Father God,

I close my eyes this morning to quiet myself and focus on You. I meditate on Your goodness, Your faithfulness, Your mercy, Your love, and Your peace. I feel Your peace saturate me. I am thankful that You will 'diffuse my soul with joy.' I am learning that our time together is teaching me Your ways. I believe that knowing Your ways and doing my best to follow them leads to blessings. I thank You for the blessings of joy, peace, and contentment in my life. I ask You to keep me in Your Presence. Remind me throughout the day that You are with me with Your blessings. I choose You today. I choose Your ways today. I choose joy today. I pray in Jesus' holy name.

Song Suggestion: I've Got Joy *by* CeCe Wynans

Love God/Love Others

"Then the righteous will answer Him saying, 'Lord, when did we see You hungry and feed You, or thirsty and give You drink? 'When did we see You a stranger and take You in, or naked and clothe You? Or when did we see You sick, or in prison, and come to You?' "And the King will answer and say to them, 'Assuredly, I say to you, inasmuch as you did it to one of the least of these My brethren, you did it to Me.'

Matthew 25:37-40 (NKJV)

Father God,

Today I come to You with thanksgiving and praise for Your love for us, all of us. I ask You to open my eyes so that I can see others the way You see them. You are generous, compassionate, merciful, and kind. Help me to be that way as well. I will purposefully live in such a way to show mercy and kindness everyday regardless of my feelings. With Your help, I can live in a way to love You and love others habitually every day. When I see someone in need, I will jump in. Even if I can only do a little bit, it will be better than doing nothing at all. I also can make plans to help others - I do not need to wait for an opportunity to pop up. I believe that You will give me opportunities and ideas. I pray that You will help me to be open and give me discernment so that I can love others in the best way possible. Thank You for Your love for me. Thank You for Your love for others.

Thank You for the days where I am in a position that I can show Your love. I pray this prayer in Jesus' name.

Song Suggestion: Give Me Your Eyes *by* Brandon Heath

Names of God

Jehovah Rapha

In Hebrew, Jehovah Rapha means The God that heals.

Saying, if you will diligently hearken to the voice of the Lord your God and will do what is right in His sight, and will listen to and obey His commandments and keep all His statutes, I will put none of the diseases upon you which I brought upon the Egyptians for I am the Lord Who heals you.

Exodus 15:26 (Amp)

Father God,

I believe You are a God who heals. I believe healing is in Your hands. I believe that You, Jesus, showed Your healing power when You healed many when You were here on the earth. Today I am coming to You with thanksgiving that You care for me and the people that are in my life. I am so grateful that You hear my prayers. I am praying specifically for… (**Note**: *Communicate to God the people in your life or who you are aware of that need God's healing power*). I am asking You for healing. I place (*names*) in the palm of Your hand and ask the Holy Spirit to give them peace and tranquility while I trust You to work in their lives. I am so amazed at Your power. As I wait for healing to occur, I give glory, honor, and praise to You as I declare that all power is in Your hands. I ask and pray these prayers in Jesus' healing name.

Song Suggestion: Healer *by* Kari Jobe

Jesus

For there is only one God, and one Mediator who can reconcile God and humanity - the man Christ Jesus. He gave his life to purchase freedom for everyone. This is the message God gave to the world at just the right time.

1 Timothy 2:5-6 (NLT)

Jesus,

I am so in awe that You would be my mediator. You stand between almighty God and me - an ordinary person trying to do my best, but always falling short of God's perfect will, Your perfect way. However, I am rejoicing and filled with gratitude for You, Who sacrificed Yourself to pay a price I could never pay. Jesus, You made me good enough so I can come to You and our Father and I can pray to You and be heard. And You help me and answer me. I am thanking You because You are praying for me still. I sit quietly and meditate on all that You have done and continue to do for me. I do not want to take what You have done for granted. Thank You for giving Your life to pay my debt, to purchase my freedom. I am overflowing with awe, praise, and gratitude to You. I pray in Jesus' redeeming name today.

Song Suggestion: Forever *by* Kari Jobe

Eternity Minded

[And indeed] the Lord will certainly deliver and draw me to Himself from every assault of evil. He will preserve and bring me safe unto His heavenly kingdom. To Him be the glory forever and ever. Amen (so be it).

2 Timothy 4:18 (Amp)

Father God,

How can I ever thank You for all the goodness, grace, mercy, and love that You pour down on me like rain? You have given me Jesus, my Savior. You have given me salvation - a life lived with You for eternity in Your heavenly kingdom. Today I read in Your Word that You will rescue me from every evil assault. You know I need a rescuer! So, I say alleluia - Praise the Lord! I praise You for Your almighty power to rescue me, change me, and take me to be with You, to be safe with You forever. I close my eyes and say, "To You be the glory forever and ever." And I offer my gratitude from deep within my heart and soul to You and only You, Father, Spirit, and Jesus. In Jesus' holy name I pray.

Song Suggestion: Tin Roof *by* Chris Tomlin with Blessing Offor

Believing

Then [the jailer] called for lights and rushed in, and trembling and terrified he fell down before Paul and Silas. And he brought them out [of the dungeon] and said, Men, what is it necessary for me to do that I may be saved? And they answered, believe in the Lord Jesus Christ [give yourself up to Him, take yourself out of your own keeping and entrust yourself into His keeping] and you will be saved [and this applies both to] you and your household as well.

Acts 16:29-31 (Amp)

Jesus,

Like the jailer, Paul, and Silas, I believe in You, in our heavenly Father and the Holy Spirit. I believe You are God's only Son. I believe You came to earth to pay the penalty for my sins. I believe You were crucified, You were buried but You came alive on the third day. I believe You were resurrected. I believe I'm now saved and set apart for You and Your purposes. I can confess my sins to You and You hear me and forgive me. I believe You are my friend and I can talk to You about all that is going on in my life. You are a God who not only saves but You want to be close to me as I communicate and live for You. I am so relieved that each day I can lean on and trust You. I am so thankful that I can 'take myself out of my own keeping and trust in You.' In this moment, I am giving up control of the chaos in my life and I am turning to You, giving it all to You.

I believe that in doing this, You will give me a richer life. In Jesus' name I pray all these things today.

Song Suggestion: God Is Able *by* Hillsong Worship and Reuben Morgan

Peace

The Lord sat as King over the deluge; the Lord [still] sits as King [and] forever! The Lord will give [unyielding and impenetrable] strength to His people; the Lord will bless His people with peace.

Psalm 29:10-11 (Amp)

Father God,

I am so thankful that I am one of Your people! I believe You are the King of kings and will be forever. I believe You have adopted me into Your family because I am a follower of Jesus, Your Son. As Your son/daughter, You have and continue to bless me. I accept Your gifts of strength and peace. I am trying to live in Your peace, learning to make peaceful decisions with what I say and do. Your peace is a gift that I accept and open intentionally each day. I praise You, Father, as the gifts of strength and peace come from You. I thank You for the gifts and blessings in my life. I especially thank You for Your peace which I breathe in this morning as I start this new day. I pray with deep appreciation for Your tranquility and peace in Jesus' name.

Song Suggestion: Always Peace *by* Brian Courtney Wilson

God's Will

"Pray, then, in this way: 'Our Father, who is in heaven, Hallowed by Your name. Your kingdom come. Your will be done, on earth as it is in heaven.

Matthew 6:9-10 (NASB)

Father God,

I have learned the prayer we know as "The Our Father" and have recited it many times but this morning I slow down and meditate on these first lines. I acknowledge and declare Your holiness. You are in heaven where everything is perfect, and You are honored and glorified continuously. I pray holy, holy, holy are You Lord and holy is Your name. I am thankful that Your kingdom is coming. I am living in Your kingdom now as I do my best to put You and Your ways first in my life. I am encouraged that Your will shall be done. You are still on Your throne, and You still have plans for Your people on earth even though we may not see them clearly. Help me to do Your will every day. Guide me, teach me, and help me to hear Your will for me. What can I do to serve You today? How can I help bring Your kingdom to my little part of the world? I declare that You are my living hope, and I am staying close to You every day as I do my best to do Your will. I pray these things in Jesus' name today.

Song Suggestion: As it is in Heaven *by* Matt Maher

Thoughts/Mindset

For the rest, brethren, whatever is true, whatever is worthy of reverence and is honorable and seemly, whatever is just, whatever is pure, whatever is lovely and lovable, whatever is kind and winsome and gracious, if there is any virtue and excellence, if there is anything worthy of praise, think on and weigh and take account of these things [fix your minds on them].

Philippians 4:8 (Amp)

Father God,

Thank You for Your direction today! Thank You that You give us the recipe for a successful, joyful life right in Your Word. Help me to think continually about Your truth, Your instructions, Your promises, Your love, and Your blessings. Remind me to think about pure, wholesome, and lovely things. When I am complaining - help me to turn it around and focus on something I am grateful for. When others hurt, disappoint, annoy, or aggravate me, give me direction, turn my thoughts to something I can praise. Oh, if I could master this concept and be consistent in my thoughts, Your joy and peace would continually surround me. Come to me, stay with me, Holy Spirit. I believe that with Your help I can become less and less like the world around me and become more like Jesus. I thank You and praise You today. I pray these things in Jesus' name.

Song Suggestion: Eyes Fixed *by* Phil Wickham

The Presence of God

One thing have I asked of the Lord, that will I seek, inquire for, and [insistently] require: that I may dwell in the house of the Lord [in His presence] all the days of my life, to behold and gaze upon the beauty [the sweet attractiveness and the delightful loveliness] of the Lord and to meditate, consider, and inquire in His temple.

Psalm 27:4 (Amp)

Father God,

Thank You for this new day. Thank You for the gift of today and the gift of getting to start over again! You know my heart, my mind and all my ways. You know how distracted I am and how easily I forget You while chasing my never ending 'to do list' in my daily life. So, I will try again today with the intention of 'dwelling in Your house all the days of my life' - of living in Your Presence all day long. I understand that I need lots of practice to improve this habit but the wonderful thing about You is that You already know that I need help and practice. You are encouraging me every day. I am humbled by Your patience, and I am so grateful for Your longsuffering. Thank You for the help that Your Holy Spirit is giving me. Please continue to nudge me further so that I can live in Your Presence more and more! I love You; I thank You and I praise You Father, Spirit, Jesus. I pray in Jesus' patient, holy name today.

Song Suggestion: He Is *by* Mark Schultz

Trust God

[Most] blessed is the man who believes in, trusts in, and relies on the Lord, and whose hope and confidence the Lord is. For he shall be like a tree planted by the waters that spreads out its roots by the river; and it shall not see and fear when heat comes; but its leaf shall be green. It shall not be anxious and full of care in the year of drought, nor shall it cease yielding fruit.

Jeremiah 17:7-8 (Amp)

Father God,

I close my eyes in this moment and visualize the beautiful picture of the scripture: a full, blooming, lush tree towering over a peaceful river lined by groves of dry and brittle trees, hanging to life. I want to be like the blooming tree: strong, confident, fed by You as I trust in You completely, no matter what happens in my life. I want to be strong, stable, and full of love completely relying on You with uncompromising trust. Help me become consistently stable in you. I still have a way to go but I am so grateful that You are still helping me to become faithfully mature. I will always be thankful for the life You are giving me. I pray in Jesus' trustworthy name this morning.

Song Suggestion: In God We Trust *by* Hillsong Worship

Forgiving

I wrote to you as I did to test you and see if you would fully comply with my instructions. When you forgive this man, I forgive him, too. And when I forgive whatever needs to be forgiven, I do so with Christ's authority for your benefit,

2 Corinthians 2:9-10 (NLT)

Father God,

Because of all You have done for me and all the mercy, forgiveness, and freedom You have given me, I am deciding to forgive all those who have hurt, betrayed, or angered me. I am letting go of the hard feelings, bitterness, grudges, and anger I have toward others. I want to live in Your joy and peace every day. I will resist holding onto unforgiveness and unforgiving thoughts and feelings. (**Note**: *Communicate to God who comes to mind that you need to forgive.*) I will lean on You for help, and I believe You will help me. I thank You now. I praise You now. I want to obey you now. I want to honor and glorify You by the way I live. I pray these things in Jesus' name.

Song Suggestion: Forgiveness *by* Matthew West

Words

Set a guard, O LORD, over my mouth; Keep watch over the door of my lips.

Psalm 141:3 (NKJV)

Father God,

I sit quietly this morning in Your Presence. I am thanking You because I have You to help me in this life. I need You to help me with hard things. I am counting on You to help me use my mouth and what I say to be a help in this world and not a hindrance. Guide me to bring light to everyone's day and not darkness. You know me so well and You know everything that I have said. You know the many, many things that I should never have said. Today I pray specifically asking You to set a guard over my mouth and keep watch over my lips. I am praying this huge prayer because I feel that You will have a full-time job with this request. I ask You to put Your hand over my mouth while patting my back gently. I am so thankful that You are with me today and every day. I am so thankful that You are helping me and guiding me. Oh, how I am depending on You as I live with the intention of using my words to please You. I ask for Your help with my words in Jesus' name.

Song Suggestion: Speak To The Mountains *by* Chris McClarney

Anxiety

If I say "My foot slips," Your mercy, O Lord, will hold me up. In the multitude of my anxieties within me, Your comforts delight my soul.

Psalm 94:18-19 (NKJV)

Father God,

You are my help when I am overwhelmed in this life. You are my tranquility when I am stressed and/or anxious. You are my peace when I am worried and fretting. I believe You are working on my behalf and I place all my anxieties in Your hands, and I accept Your comfort. Help me to quiet myself and get connected to You and remember that You are with me. I remember all the times that You have helped me and gotten me back on track. Thank You for being compassionate with me, thank You for Your loving kindness. Thank You for being my comfort and joy. You are strengthening me on this chaotic journey of life with all its ups and downs. Thank You for being by my side. I am so relieved that You are here with me. I breathe in Your stillness and peace, and I breathe out my love, my gratitude, my praise to You today. I pray in Jesus' comforting name.

Song Suggestion: Gonna Be Alright *by* Ryan Ellis

Thankful

You must each decide in your heart how much to give. And don't give reluctantly or in response to pressure. "For God loves a person who gives cheerfully. And God will generously provide all you need. Then you will always have everything you need and plenty left over to share with others.

2 Corinthians 9:7-8 (NKJV)

Father God,

Thank You so much for Your grace. You pour favor and blessings on me even though I do not deserve it. You give me everything I need, and I open my hands and receive all blessings and favor with thanksgiving and praise. May I live my life remembering and being grateful for Your abundant grace, favor, and blessings. May Your kindness and goodness flow out of my hand to all those around me. I am so thankful that I have opportunities to be an abundant giver so that my life, attitude, and service gives You glory. Thank You, thank You, thank You for Your blessings that are reigning down on me. In Jesus' name I pray this grateful prayer.

Song Suggestion: All to You *by* Lincoln Brewster

Prayer

So let us come boldly to the throne of our gracious God. There we will receive his mercy, and we will find grace to help us when we need it most.

Hebrews 4:16 (NLT)

Father God,

I boldly come to Your throne this morning with so much gratitude in my heart because I can come to You with ALL my 'baggage,' and You accept me and listen to me with grace and mercy. Even though I have sinned, You still open Your arms to me. I can come to You with my requests, and You will be with me in my time of need. I take a moment now to pray for others as well as for myself. (**Note**: *Communicate your special needs and requests.*) Thank You for Your amazing grace and for listening to my prayers and for all You are doing for me, the seen and the unseen. I rely on You Lord. I trust in You. I am leaning on You, and I am forever thanking and praising You. In Jesus' name I pray today.

Song Suggestion: Holy Water *by* We the Kingdom

Seek God

Seek the LORD while He may be found; call upon Him while He is near.

Isaiah 55:6 (NASB)

Father God,

I am seeking You this morning. I am calling on Your holy name. I am not going to wait until I am perfect. I admit that there are many times in my day where I go my own way and I forget that I am Your child. I thank You that I can run back to You and You always show me mercy and compassion. You are mighty in Your steadfastness, longsuffering, and patience with me. As I seek You in this moment, I bow down before You - the almighty, majestic Lord of all. I thank You, praise you and give You honor and glory today while I am seeking You. I sit quietly for a few minutes this morning to just be with You. In Jesus' name I pray.

Song Suggestion: Call upon the Lord (Live) *by* Elevation Worship

Discouragement

I am the Door; anyone who enters in through Me will be saved (will live). He will come in and he will go out [freely] and will find pasture. The thief comes only in order to steal and kill and destroy. I came that they may have and enjoy life, and have it in abundance (to the full, till it overflows).

John 10:9-10 (Amp)

Jesus,

There is always something in my life to cause me to be discouraged, disillusioned, disappointed, discontent. You have told us that it will always be this way as the devil comes to 'steal, kill and destroy.' But You came to give me life - an abundant life. I am choosing to focus on You. I am choosing to follow You and put You first in my life so that my life will be overflowing with You. I will focus my thoughts, not on all that is wrong or all that disappoints me, but I will focus on the things that You have done and continue to do for me. I will focus on living with more peace, forgiveness, compassion, and love - the way that You lived. I will enjoy my life as I seek and focus on You. I will thank You, praise You, and live to honor You every day. I believe that my discouragement will diminish as I live Your way. I pray this prayer in Your holy name, Jesus.

Song Suggestion: Abundantly More *by* North Point Worship feat. Seth Condrey

God's Love

But God is so rich in mercy, and he loved us so much, that even though we were dead because of our sins, he gave us life when he raised Christ from the dead. (It is only by God's grace that you have been saved!)

Ephesians 2:4-5 (NLT)

Father God,

I am so thankful that You are a God who loves me. You loved me before I was paying any attention to You. You loved me when I was ignoring You and doing everything my own way. You continue to love me even though sometimes I am unfaithful to You, sometimes I am self-centered and selfish and sometimes I am unkind. But Your grace, mercy and love endure. I am profoundly grateful for Your grace that saved me. In this moment, I meditate on the new life that You have given me, and I set my intention to let Your love be reflected in the way that I think and behave. I am so thankful for Your great and wonderful love. In Jesus' name I pray today.

Song Suggestion: Oh But God *by* The Worship Initiative feat Shane and Shane

Hope

Not lagging in diligence, fervent in spirit, serving the Lord; rejoicing in hope, patient in tribulation, continuing steadfastly in prayer;

Romans 12:11-12 (NKJV)

Father God,

Thank You for Your Word which guides the choices I make. Today I pray that You will open my heart and mind today. I pray that You will help me to be passionate about Your truths and Your ways. Help me to be diligent, steadfast, and stable. Help me to serve You better - open my eyes to the opportunities and needs of those around me. As I live my life in service to You, I will rejoice in Your hope. I will do my best to be patient during times of tribulation and I will continue to pray. I believe that You will guide me on this journey. I believe that You will fill me with Your peace and hope. A peace and hope that never ends. I am so grateful that no matter what my circumstances are - You are my hope, and You will remain. I pray in Jesus' name today.

Song Suggestion: You Keep Hope Alive *by* Jon Reddick and Mandisa

Perseverance

Dear brothers and sisters, when troubles come your way, consider it an opportunity for great joy. For you know that when your faith is tested, your endurance has a chance to grow. So let it grow, for when your endurance is fully developed, you will be perfect and complete, needing nothing.

James 1:2-4 (NLT)

Father God,

Thank You that You are always by my side. You have said that I will have trouble in my life (not if but when). As I have hardships and difficult times in my life, I will get to experience Your comfort and Your compassion. The more I lean on, trust in and hope in You I will experience more of Your goodness. As I experience You more, You will infuse into me Your spiritual gifts. Oh, how grateful I am because I have You to support me and to give me strength, courage, and endurance. How grateful I am to get to experience Your grace, compassion, goodness, and Your love. I believe that alongside You, I can persevere. I will not give up. I will focus on You for the rest of my days. I pray in Jesus' name today.

Song Suggestion: I Won't Let Go *by* Rascal Flatts

I am a Child of God

For all who are led by the Spirit of God are children of God. So you have not received a spirit that makes you fearful slaves. Instead you received God's Spirit when he adopted you as his own children. Now we call him, "Abba, Father."

Romans 8:14-15 (NLT)

Father God,

I am different - I want to be different from everyone who lives day to day on their own. I want to be led by Your Spirit. I take this moment to declare that You are my Father and I want to live close to You and I want to depend on You. I accept the spiritual gifts that You give me as Your son/daughter. The gift of trusting in You and living without fear of judgment and condemnation; The gift of joy, knowing that I have been adopted into Your family; The gift of peace and hope as I learn to trust in You more. So, I take my stand and align myself with You Father, Jesus, and Holy Spirit. For I am a child of God. I gratefully pray this prayer in Jesus' name.

Song Suggestion: Abba (Live) *by* The Worship Initiative feat. Davy Flowers

Motivation

So don't make judgments about anyone ahead of time - before the Lord returns. For he will bring our darkest secrets to light and will reveal our private motives. Then God will give to each one whatever praise is due.

1 Corinthians 4:5 (NLT)

Father God,

You know the motives of my heart. This morning, I want to ask You to help me understand my own motives. Why do I do the things I do? Do I put You first in my life? Do I take time to focus on You and stay close to You? Are you my first thought or an afterthought? The truth is You are a faithful, loving, unbelievably merciful God who knows me inside and out. I ask You to shine Your light on me and help me to know You better, live nearer to You daily and help increase my motivation to discipline myself so that I am following You and Your ways. While You are working with me, I will be praying to You and thanking You for pulling me out of darkness and giving me a beautiful life. In Jesus' name I pray.

Song Suggestion: Jesus, Friend of Sinners *by* Casting Crowns

Pray for Others

The Lord is not slack concerning His promise, as some count slackness, but is longsuffering toward us, not willing that any should perish but that all should come to repentance.

2 Peter 3:9 (NKJV)

Father God,

Thank You for Your promises. Thank You for Your patience with us. Thank You that You do not want any people to perish but You want us all to have eternal life with You. You have given all of us freedom to choose. I choose You. I believe in You and Your promises. This morning, I pray for … (**Note**: *Communicate to God anyone by name that You know does not have a personal relationship with Him.*) I pray that You will give those whom I have named, wisdom and vision to understand Your saving Grace. I pray that they will understand how good, how faithful, how loving You are. I pray that they will yearn for Your joy, Your peace, Your hope in their lives. I believe You are working on their hearts even if I do not see any changes. I believe that You will act at the most appropriate time. I thank You for all You are doing on (*name's*) behalf. I thank You for all You are doing in my life as well. I pray in Jesus' saving name this morning.

Song Suggestion: What Faith Can Do *by* Kutless

I am... A New Creation

Therefore if any person is [ingrafted] in Christ (the Messiah) he is a new creation (a new creature altogether); the old [previous moral and spiritual condition] has passed away. Behold, the fresh and new has come!

2 Corinthians 5:17 (Amp)

Father God,

Today is a new day to start over again! I am so grateful and blessed to get to start it with You right now. You have made me new, and even though I may feel the same, I believe I have new opportunities and new options that are opening for me. I can choose Your life-filled thoughts instead of my old self-defeating or worrisome ones. I can choose to use my words to encourage and lift everyone I talk to rather than complain and 'react' verbally to all of life's unfortunate circumstances. I can choose forgiveness rather than being offended. I can choose Your peace and I can put my trust in You when I am starting to experience anger, bitterness, disappointments, and anxiety. Oh, I have all these new options for me now that I am a new creation. I am grateful that You are awakening me so that I can live the best life possible. I pray with deep gratitude in Jesus' name.

Song Suggestion: Beautiful *by* Bethany Dillon

I Will...

But be doers of the Word [obey the message], and not merely listeners to it, betraying yourselves [into deception by reasoning contrary to the Truth].

James 1:22 (Amp)

Father God,

Thank You for giving us Your instructions found in Your Word. I ask You to help me follow Your ways every day. I am deciding right now at this moment that I will be a 'doer of the Word;' I will obey the message as best as I can. There are so many things that I need to change, so many ways where I tend to get off Your path. It is easy to get overwhelmed and do nothing. But today I ask You to show me one thing - just one thing that I can do to obey You, to follow You. Then I will do whatever it takes to do Your will more consistently. Once I have success in that area, I am asking You to show me another thing! I believe that over time, I will become more like You! I believe You are helping me. I welcome Your direction and Your instruction. I thank You for Your Word which is consistent and true. I thank You for Your patience and mercy while I try to learn of all Your ways. I praise You because You are so good and kind to me as I try to submit to You. I pray this prayer in Jesus' name.

Song Suggestion: Send Me (Live) *by* Jenn Johnson feat Chris Quilala

September 1

Holy Sovereign God

THE LORD reigns, He is clothed with majesty; the Lord is robed. He has girded Himself with strength and power; the world also is established, that it cannot be moved. Your throne is established from of old; You are from everlasting.

Psalm 93:1-2 (Amp)

Father God,

You are our everlasting God, full of strength and majesty that we cannot truly understand. I thank You and praise You for all that You are. I choose to lean into Your strength because I need You every day. I am nothing and can do nothing significant without You. I am relieved that You are reigning over us. As our world is getting further and further away from You and as we see chaos all around, it is comforting to know that You are still on the throne. Your strength and power will last forever. Help me remember how holy, how powerful, how everlasting You are. As I sit here right now, I can see through my eyes of faith that I am surrounded by Your majesty, Your love, Your grace. I bow down before You, my holy sovereign Father. In Jesus' name I pray.

Song Suggestion: You Reign *by* MercyMe

Praise

And he said: "The LORD is my rock and my fortress and my deliverer; the God of my strength, in whom I will trust; my shield and the horn of my salvation, my stronghold and my refuge; my Savior, You save me from violence. I will call upon the LORD, who is worthy to be praised; so shall I be saved from my enemies.

2 Samuel 22:2-4 (NKJV)

Father God,

Thank You for being the God Who saves. You have saved me on so many levels. Thank You for being my rock, the One I can build my life upon. As I live Your way, seeking to do Your will, You bless me with joy, peace, and love. When things don't go as I would like, I can run to You and You comfort and counsel me. When I go off on my own to do what I want, You have a plan to save me. I am saved forever because of all that You have done. You are my Savior, You are my refuge, You are my help. You are faithful and You keep picking me up, brushing me off, and helping me to start over again. Because of this, I bow before You with empty hands and say thank You. I praise You, You are worthy of praise. In Jesus' name I pray today.

Song Suggestion: Worthy Of My Song *by* Maverick City Music feat Phil Wickham and Chandler Moore

Wisdom

If you are wise and understand God's ways, prove it by living an honorable life, doing good works with the humility that comes from wisdom.

James 3:13 (NLT)

Father God,

I come with an open, grateful heart this morning. I am thanking You for giving me opportunities to learn and understand Your ways. I ask You today to teach me the wisdom of Your ways and Your truth. Thank You for leading me. I invite You to ignite a passion in me to help others with gentleness and humility. I invite You to pour Your wisdom down on me today. As I follow You and Your pure ways, I am so thankful that I am growing closer to You. I pray all these things in Jesus' name today.

Song Suggestion: Audience of One *by* Big Daddy Weave

September 4

Forgiven

If My people, who are called by My name, shall humble themselves, pray, seek, crave, and require of necessity My face and turn from their wicked ways, then will I hear from heaven, forgive their sin and heal their land.

2 Chronicles 7:14 (Amp)

Father God,

I am so thankful that You are teaching me Your ways as I seek You. I want more of You in my life. Help me to learn to humble myself, to crave You, to require, and need You.

Guide me so I do not go back to my independent ways, where I live my life without You. I am so thankful that You hear me when I pray. I am so thankful that You are a God who listens, who forgives and who heals. I believe I am forgiven because of what Jesus did for me on the cross. I am forever in debt because I owe all to You and Jesus. Thank You for Your forgiveness. Thank You for Your healing powers in my life. Thank You for adopting me into Your family. I can now live forgiven, with no shame, guilt, or condemnation. I can now live for You! I pray with deep gratitude and praise in Jesus' name.

Song Suggestion: Healing Has Begun *by* Matthew West

Open Ears

So faith comes from hearing, that is, hearing the Good News about Christ.

Romans 10:17 (NLT)

Father God,

Thank You for allowing me to hear and understand the message of Jesus. Thank You for opening my heart and mind so that I have faith in You. Faith in the Good News. Faith that You are always with me, that You help and guide me, that You are for me and not against me, that You give me peace, love, comfort, and joy. Faith that You have saved me. Continue to open my ears to Your messages so that I can learn so much more about You and then I can get closer and closer to You each day. I ask You to help me see and hear You more clearly. I pray with thanksgiving and praise in Jesus' holy name today.

Song Suggestion: SMS (Shine) *by* David Crowder Band

Joy

This is the day which the Lord has made; let's rejoice and be glad in it.

Psalm 118:24 (NASB)

Father God,

Thank You for this day. Thank You for the sun coming up and bringing us light. Thank You that Your light shines all around me all day long. Thank You for each breath I take. I purposefully choose to be thankful today. I purposefully choose to focus on joyous things. Trials and tribulations may try to derail me, but I will bring my thoughts back to You and the joy of living my life with You. I will rejoice on purpose all day long. I will be Your joy today. In Jesus' name I pray this prayer.

Song Suggestion: Today is the Day *by* Lincoln Brewster

Love God/Love Others

After washing their feet, he put on his robe again and sat down and asked, "Do you understand what I was doing? You call me 'Teacher' and 'Lord,' and you are right, because that's what I am. And since I, your Lord and Teacher, have washed your feet, you ought to wash each other's feet. I have given you an example to follow. Do as I have done to you.

John 13:12-15 (NLT)

Father God,

Thank You for sending Jesus not only to be my Savior but my teacher and example as well. While I may not have the opportunity to wash feet, I am sure there are many other things I can do to show Your love, to help others. Help me see these opportunities. Help me be generous with all I have. Help me to be humble so that I am up for any task that needs to get done. I will ask the Holy Spirit daily, "What can I do to show Your love today?" I will show my love to You by showing love to others. I pray this prayer with praise in Jesus' name.

Song Suggestion: Less Like Me *by* Zach Williams

Names of God

Jehovah Shalom

Shalom refers to soundness, completeness, harmony, and the absence of strife: The Lord is Peace.

Then the LORD said to him, "Peace be with you; do not fear, you shall not die." So Gideon built an altar there to the LORD, and called it The-LORD-Is-Peace. To this day it is still in Ophrah of the Abiezrites.

Judges 6:23-24 (NKJV)

Father God,

I believe You are Peace. Jesus has given me peace as He said, "I leave you my peace." I take time this morning to meditate on this peace and let Your peace saturate all of me. When I am with You during our quiet times, I am complete in Your peaceful Presence.

Help me to stay in peace when I go into the world and face strife, fears, and anxieties. Help me remember I have Your peace within me. Guide me in the willful act of activating this peace I possess when I encounter trials and stress. I thank You for this amazing gift of Your peace. I thank You that You are Jehovah Shalom - a God full of unshakeable peace. I pray this prayer in Jesus' name this morning.

Song Suggestion: Shalom *by* Bridge Worship feat Selnick Sene

September 9

Jesus

MY LITTLE children, I write you these things so that you may not violate God's law and sin. But if anyone should sin, we have an Advocate (One Who will intercede for us) with the Father - [it is] Jesus Christ [the all] righteous [upright, just, Who conforms to the Father's will in every purpose, thought and action].

1 John 2:1 (Amp)

Father God,

Thank You for sending us Jesus. Thank You for giving us an eternal hope. Jesus, thank You for being my advocate in addition to being my Savior. I need both a Savior and an advocate. I need You to intercede for me all the time. Although I try to do Your will, I often do not. I often fall short. But that is why You came; this is why I need You. I can fall on You Jesus. You repeatedly pick me up, clean me up and send me on my way. You are full of grace, mercy, and love. I will continue to gratefully lean on You and trust You to guide me on this journey with You. So, in this moment, I gather my love, gratitude, praise and send them to You. You deserve it all. I pray all these things with deep gratitude and love in Jesus' name.

Song Suggestion: One and Only Jesus *by* Vertical Worship

Eternity Minded

"I tell you the truth, those who listen to my message and believe in God who sent me have eternal life. They will never be condemned for their sins, but they have already passed from death into life.

John 5:24 (NLT)

Father God,

I have heard, I have read Your Word and I believe in what it says. Jesus, I believe in You and that You came to give me eternal life. I am building my life on You because You are my life giver. I am working towards putting my complete trust in You and not in my own plans or my manipulative actions or the economy or the government or anyone or anything else - only You. And when I stumble in my faith, I believe that You will pick me up and set me straight again. You will not condemn or judge, but You help me to try again. I love this life with You. I thank You that I have already passed from death into life. With great joy, I anticipate spending eternity with You in a new world surrounded by Your love and light. I pray with eternal gratitude and praise in Jesus' name.

Song Suggestion: Heaven Changes Everything *by* Big Daddy Weave

September 11

Believing

But because Jesus lives forever, his priesthood lasts forever. Therefore he is able, once and forever, to save those who come to God through him. He lives forever to intercede with God on their behalf.

Hebrews 7:24-25 (NLT)

Jesus,

Thank You for being the God Who saves, the God Who laid down Your life for me, and the God Who intercedes and intervenes on my behalf with our almighty Father. You are amazing for all that You are, for all that You have done and for all You continue to do. I reach deep within me, and I abandon my heart and soul and give them to You, right now in this moment. Teach me what surrendering to You looks like. I know You are holding my hand (spiritually) and Your Spirit is filling me. As I move forward into this day, I ask that You remind me to come back to this moment and refill myself with You. I pray in Jesus' saving name today.

Song Suggestion: Because He Lives (Amen) *by* Matt Maher

Peace

Therefore let us pursue the things which make for peace and the things by which one may edify another.

Romans 14:19 (NKJV)

Father God,

I start my day giving You thanks and praise. This morning, I read that You want me to live my life day by day in a peaceful way. I am meditating on Your peaceful ways this morning so that I can go out into the world and behave in a peaceful way that will please You. I take some quiet moments to reflect on ways I can improve in this area. (**Note**: *Communicate to God what comes to mind or ask God to communicate to you times when you could have made peaceful choices.*) I am so thankful that You are teaching me Your ways of tranquility and peace because Your way is the best way and will result in an elevated life for me. I have a long way to go but day by day, I am growing closer to You and learning more from You. Thank You for these opportunities to grow. I praise, bless, and honor You today, Father, Spirit, and Jesus who is the Prince of Peace. I pray all these things in Jesus' name.

Song Suggestion: Peace *by* Danny Gokey

September 13

God's Will

For we are His workmanship, created in Christ Jesus for good works, which God prepared beforehand so that we would walk in them.

Ephesians 2:10 (NASB)

Father God,

Everything I do today, I will do for You. I will be encouraging and patient with my family. I will be kind and helpful to my coworkers/peers. I will be friendly and merciful to strangers. I will drive carefully, tolerant of other drivers, I will not be the one making angry accusations. I will smile, wave, and greet my neighbors as friends. I will welcome my household chores and work assignments with a good attitude. I will do my best at whatever task is in front of me. All day, I will seek opportunities to honor You. I give You thanks for helping me to see any opportunity that comes along. I will trust You to guide me every day. Empty me of selfishness and fill me with an attitude of service so I can do Your will. I pray in Jesus' holy name today.

Song Suggestion: Empty Me *by* Jeremy Camp

Thoughts/Mindset

Fulfill my joy by being like-minded, having the same love, being of one accord, of one mind.

Philippians 2:2 (NKJV)

Father God,

I come to You this morning with thanks and praise for Your teachings. I thank You and praise You for Your ways. I thank You and praise You for the opportunity to learn from Jesus. I ask You to help me have the mind of Jesus. If only Your church could be more like-minded and more loving, this world would be a better place. I cannot change the world, but I can work on myself with Your help. So, help me change my thoughts. Help me to amend my thoughts so that I am less focused on me and more focused on You and on others. When I am angry, help me turn my thoughts to forgiveness and mercy. When I am feeling lonely, change my thoughts to how I can reach out to others. When I am overwhelmed, guide my thoughts to remember that Your peace is within me. When I am fearful, influence my thoughts to remind me that You are with me in all Your power and majesty. Let Your thoughts permeate my mind, heart, and soul and guide me to join others in our quest to show Your love. I pray all these things in Jesus' name.

Song Suggestion: Man in the Mirror *by* Michael Jackson

September 15

The Presence of God

Create in me a clean heart, O God, and renew a right, persevering and steadfast spirit within me. Cast me not away from Your presence and take not Your Holy Spirit from me.

Psalm 51:10-11 (Amp)

Father God,

You are my Creator, and You created me in Your image. You continue to mold me and guide me to have the mind of Christ which is holy and pure. I ask You to continue to create in me a clean, pure heart. I need You to help me persist in my endeavors toward living in Your Presence. Help me pursue these lofty goals that sometimes feel insurmountable. In the light of Your constant help, I will focus each day praising You more, worshiping You more, thanking You more, praying to You more, trusting in You more each day. I believe Your Presence is with me and will not leave me on my own. I thank You for not giving up on me. I give You my thanks and praise for continually guiding me closer to You. I pray all these things in Jesus' name today.

Song Suggestion: Breathe *by* Michael W. Smith

September 16

Trust God

The L*ORD says, "I will guide you along the best pathway for your life. I will advise you and watch over you. Do not be like a senseless horse or mule that needs a bit and bridle to keep it under control." Many sorrows come to the wicked, but unfailing love surrounds those who trust the* L*ORD.*

Psalm 32:8-10 (NLT)

Father God,

This morning, I sit in quiet wonder as I meditate on Your compassion and loving kindness. I let them shine in, on and all around me like rays of sunshine through the trees. I soak in Your deep, unending love and I let it radiate through me. I am full of love and gratitude for You. I continue to increase my willingness to trust You in all areas of my life including my relationships, my finances, my dreams and goals, my work/school life, my spiritual growth, my health. If there is an area in my life that I have not trusted to You, I ask You to tell me and help me surrender that area to You. I believe You are trustworthy and I can put my hope in You. I praise You and thank You for Your faithfulness and Your patience with me. I pray in Jesus' name today.

Song Suggestion: Trust In You *by* Lauren Daigle

Forgiving

He who covers a transgression seeks love, but he who repeats a matter separates friends.

Proverbs 17:9 (NKJV)

Father God,

You are a God who forgives. You have shown Your love for me by forgiving me over and over again. I seek a forgiving attitude like Yours. Help me to cover others' mistakes and errors. Help me to keep my judgments and my comments to myself. I believe Your grace has covered me even though I do not always deserve it and I in turn am learning to give grace to others, even if I think they don't deserve it. Help me to live like You: giving love, giving mercy, giving grace, and giving forgiveness quickly and easily. I believe this is Your way, Jesus, thank You for Your example. Thank You for Your words of life. Thank You for forgiving me first, so I can forgive others and live an abundant, spirit filled life. I pray this prayer in Jesus' name today.

Song Suggestion: Don't Believe Them *by* Lauren Daigle

September 18

My Words

Do all things without complaining and disputing, that you may become blameless and harmless, children of God without fault in the midst of a crooked and perverse generation among whom you shine as lights in the world,

Philippians 2:14-15 (NKJV)

Father God,

Oh, how I want to be Your bright light in a dark world. Oh, how I want to live for and please You. I read in Your Word today that I cannot please You if I am complaining and arguing. I am sitting quietly in Your Presence this morning and asking You to make me more aware of my attitude and my words of complaint so I can stop! Complaining and arguing is filtering my light. I am deciding that I want to live as a beacon of light which means I am creating light and life with my words. I will lean on Your guidance. I will be thankful and say so rather than focus and complain about circumstances. I will get up every day and renew my commitment to live a life without murmuring or questioning You. I will praise and thank You and dedicate my mouth/my words to You each day. Help me, help me, Lord. I pray all these things in Jesus' name today.

Song Suggestion: Good Day *by* Forrest Frank

Anxiety

For God did not give us a spirit of timidity (of cowardice, of craven and cringing and fawning fear), but [He has given us a spirit] of power and of love and of calm and well-balanced mind and discipline and self-control.

2 Timothy 1:7 (Amp)

God My Father,

Thank You so much for the gifts You give me. The scripture today says that You have given me a spirit of power, of love, of calm. You have given me a well-balanced mind, discipline, and self-control. I honestly do not always feel these gifts. Sometimes I allow myself to get overwhelmed with feelings of fear and anxiety and total loss of all control. So, this morning I am grateful that I can be open and honest with You as You are my Father who knows me, knows my weaknesses, and loves me anyway. I submit my feelings of fear and anxiety to You in this moment. I meditate and take time to think about and try to dig deep and connect with these spiritual gifts of power, love, calm, discipline, and self-control. I ask You to help me internalize and use these gifts to a greater degree than I currently do. I believe I can rise above my anxieties and my fears with Your help. I pray for all these things in Jesus' peaceful name.

Song Suggestion: Be Still *by* Hillsong Worship

Thankful

Oh, how great is Your goodness, which You have laid up for those who fear, revere, and worship You, goodness which You have wrought for those who trust and take refuge in You before the sons of men!

Psalm 31:19 (Amp)

Father God,

How great You are. How great is Your goodness toward me. I am meditating on all the blessings in my life. (**Note**: *Communicate to God the personal blessings that come to mind.*) You have given me these blessings. All good things come from You. I am so, so grateful and I am pouring out my gratitude to You now. I will meditate and think about my blessings throughout the day so that my prayers of gratitude will flow from me to You all day long. In Jesus' name I pray this morning.

Song Suggestion: God You're so Good (Live) *by* Passion, Kristian Stanfill Feat. Melodie Malone

Prayer

The Lord *is near to all who call upon Him, to all who call upon Him in truth. He will fulfill the desire of those who fear Him; He also will hear their cry and save them.*

Psalm 145:18-19 (NKJV)

Father God,

I believe You are THE living God who listens and who hears me. I love that I can come to You anytime, all day and/or all night and You are near to me, You are attentive to me. I am sorry to say that I am not as attentive to You, but I am working toward living in Your Presence more consistently. Right now, I am praying that I will hear You, that I will have a heart and mind of obedience, that my desire to be with You more will grow. I worship You now and I thank you because You are a God Who saves. You have saved me, and I belong to You. Thank You for hearing my prayers, Father. Thank You that my prayers are not in vain. I pray today in Your Son, Jesus' name.

Song Suggestion: Pray *by* Sanctus Real

September 22

Seek God

Let all those that seek and require You rejoice and be glad in You; let such as love Your salvation say continually, The Lord be magnified! [As for me] I am poor and needy, yet the Lord takes thought and plans for me. You are my Help and my Deliverer. O my God, do not tarry!

Psalm 40:16-17 (Amp)

Father God,

As I seek You this morning, I realize that I am not alone. You are always with me. I can sigh in relief because You are here. You take care of me. I relax as I think about all my daily tasks and stressors. I can say, "I am magnifying the Lord today because You are my help, You are my rescuer." I am joyful as I praise You and rely on You all day today. Sitting quietly, I start my day breathing in the fact that I do not need to worry because You are taking care of things, and I can let go of all negative thoughts. I breathe them out and I breathe You in. Thank You, thank You for all Your thoughts and plans that You have for me. I am filled with gratitude for the peace that seeking You brings. In Jesus' name I pray today.

Song Suggestion: Christ Be Magnified *by* Cody Carnes

Discouragement

Many are they who say of me, "There is no help for him in God." Selah
But You, O LORD, are a shield for me, my glory and the One who lifts up my head. I cried to the LORD with my voice, and He heard me from His holy hill. Selah
I lay down and slept; I awoke, for the LORD sustained me.

Psalm 3:2-5 (NKJV)

Father God,

When I am tired and weary, I cry out to You. I am discouraged, discontented, and disappointed. I am… (**Note**: *Communicate to God any feelings that You are having and why*). I am grateful that You hear me. Jesus, You have been deeply discouraged and disappointed with people in Your life so I know that You are a Lord who understands. I believe You will give me rest. As I share my burdens with You and allow You to carry them, You will help me replace my sadness with peace. I believe You are sustaining me and You will restore me. You are the One who lifts my head, You are my help in my times of trouble. You are my shield. I am resting in You right now. I am giving You all my disappointments and pain. I am letting them go. I am trusting that You will work all things out for good. You are a good and wonderful Father. I thank You and praise You for all You are. In Jesus' name I pray.

Song Suggestion: God Is In This Story *by* Katy Nichole and Big Daddy Weave

God's Love

God showed how much he loved us by sending his one and only Son into the world so that we might have eternal life through him. This is real love- not that we loved God, but that he loved us and sent his Son as a sacrifice to take away our sins.

1 John 4:9-10 (NLT)

Father God,

Thank You for showing me Your love. You have loved me since You created me, and You have watched me grow. You were my Father then and You are my Father now. I am so grateful that You made a way for me to spend eternity with You. You have given me life here and now and You promise me life in the future with You. I let Your love permeate my mind, my heart, and soul in this moment and I meditate on the cost of Your love, the sacrifice that both You and Jesus made. I carry Your love with me as I move into this day. I am profoundly grateful, and full of love and gratitude for You. I pray with praise in the name of Jesus,' my Savior.

Song Suggestion: Love Song *by* Third Day

September 25

Hope

UNTO YOU, O Lord, do I bring my life. O my God I trust, lean on, rely on, and am confident in You. Let me not be put to shame or [my hope in You] be disappointed; let not my enemies triumph over me. Yes, let none who trust and wait hopefully and look for You be put to shame or be disappointed; let them be ashamed who forsake the right or deal treacherously without cause.

Psalm 25:1-3 (Amp)

Father God,

This world we live in is noisy and chaotic, but nothing in this world can replace You in my life. I close my eyes this morning and intentionally bring You my life. I trust You, lean on You, and rely on You. You are my hope and I need You every minute. I love this time together where I can step away from the world and the circumstances in my life and focus on You. I am always full of hope that You will send Your light, Your truth directly to me so that I can follow You. I believe You will show me Your ways and teach me Your paths. I am choosing to anchor my hope in You. I will praise You; I will serve You; I will worship You while I live my life in an attitude of hope and trust. I pray all these things in Jesus' name.

Song Suggestion: My Hope Is You *by* Third Day

September 26

Perseverance

And I am certain that God, who began the good work within you, will continue his work until it is finally finished on the day when Christ Jesus returns.

Philippians 1:6 (NLT)

Father God,

I am so thankful that You are working in me. Sometimes Your work seems so slow that I wonder if anything is happening and other times, I can see that I am slowly learning, growing, and changing. Help me to be persistent in my desire to live in Your Presence and to please You. I believe You are helping me become all You want me to be. I believe You are changing me from the inside out. I believe You are good and that You are good to me. Thank You for guiding me every day. Thank You for giving me the internal motivation and persistence to get up each day and continue to do the good work that You have planned for me. Someday, Jesus will come back, and I want to hear You say that I have been a good and faithful servant. I pray this prayer in Jesus' holy name today.

Song Suggestion: Getting Started *by* Jeremy Camp

I am a Child of God

But when the proper time had fully come, God sent His Son, born of a woman, born subject to [the regulations of] the Law, to purchase the freedom of (to ransom, to redeem, to atone for) those who were subject to the Law, that we might be adopted and have sonship conferred upon us [and be recognized as God's sons].

Galatians 4:4-5 (Amp)

Father God,

I sit quietly in Your Presence this morning and think about all You have done for me. You sent Your Son to earth - He left Your side in heaven with a specific purpose in mind: to make it possible so that we might be adopted by You. I thank You for Your plan and the incomprehensible cost to You. I thank Jesus for coming to us and for taking our sins away at a traumatic cost to Him. I offer profound thanksgiving that I am adopted and am recognized as Your son/daughter. I often take this for granted but today I ponder this gift. I want to praise You and thank You for adopting me. I recognize and declare that You are an amazing Father. I believe You want what is best for me and You are showering me with love, blessings, and favor. I ask that You help me continue to live like Your child so that I can make You proud of me. I pray all these things in Jesus' redeeming name.

Song Suggestion: Miracle Child *by* Brandon Lake

Motivation

But I, the LORD, search all hearts and examine secret motives. I give all people their due rewards, according to what their actions deserve."

Jeremiah 17:10 (NLT)

Father God,

You are the omniscient, all-knowing, ever-present God. You reward those who are living to please You. You know my mind and my heart. As I journey along with You, I am learning (albeit very slowly) that Your ways are best. I ask You to help purify my mind and heart. It is only You who can help me change - help me be more like You. Empower me to continue to love You, myself, and others more. Help me continue to be patient, to be kind and to be compassionate to myself and others. Empower me to continue to be content and thankful for You and for all You have blessed me with. Guide me to purposefully walk beside You every day. Purify my motives so that my thoughts and actions are to please You, not myself or other people. Fill me with a passion for You and Your thoughts and attitudes. Thank You for moving me forward. I am so dependent on You. I pray with praise and gratitude this morning in Jesus' name.

Song Suggestion: Awaken *by* Natalie Grant

Pray for Others

Let all the world look to me for salvation! For I am God; there is no other. I have sworn by my own name; I have spoken the truth, and I will never go back on my word: Every knee will bend to me, and every tongue will confess allegiance to me."

Isaiah 45:22-23 (NLT)

Father God,

I believe You are the one true God, the God Who saves. I am so thankful that You are a God who wants to be close to me. I pray for others this morning who are not yet close to You, for those who have not turned to You to be saved. Specifically, I pray for… (**Note**: *Communicate to God those who are on your mind*). I ask that You help them to turn to You. Clear their vision, soften their hearts, refute their arguments somehow. Help them see that You are the one, true, holy, and perfect God. Help them join me in bending their knees and confessing belief and allegiance to You now, while we are all here living on earth. Help us all learn more of You and Your perfect and loving ways. I pray now with all that is within me. I pray with praise and thanksgiving that You are the God Who saves and will continue to save until Jesus returns. I pray in Jesus' name today.

Song Suggestion: Love Has Come *by* Mark Schultz

I am... Free

There is therefore now no condemnation to those who are in Christ Jesus, who do not walk according to the flesh, but according to the Spirit. For the law of the Spirit of life in Christ Jesus has made me free from the law of sin and death.

Romans 8:1-2 (NKJV)

Father God,

Thank You for Your mercy, compassion, and love. Thank You that I am free from condemnation. I no longer need to feel guilty for my weaknesses and sins. You are not mad at me. You are patient with me and will show me my sins. As I learn of my wrongdoings, I can apologize and start over again. I can move forward with You by my side. Jesus, You have given me the Spirit of Life. I am free from sin and death. I am free to live a joyful, loving, generous life for You! I am free to enjoy the gifts You have given me. I am free to run to You and embrace Your peace, tranquility, and calmness. I am free to live and to love. I contemplate this freedom right now in this moment. Help me remember that I can live in this freedom every minute of every day. I pray this prayer with deep gratitude and praise in Jesus' name.

Song Suggestion: I Am Free *by* Desperation Band

Holy Sovereign God

HANNAH PRAYED, and said, my heart exults and triumphs in the Lord; my horn (my strength) is lifted up in the Lord. My mouth is no longer silent, for it is opened wide over my enemies, because I rejoice in Your salvation. There is none holy like the Lord, there is none besides You; there is no Rock like our God.

1 Samuel 2:1-2 (Amp)

Father God,

You are our holy, holy Lord. I thank You that You are my salvation. You have made a way that I can be with You, wrapped in Your love, wrapped in Your light forever. I choose to rejoice as I think about all You have done. I rejoice that You are my God, my rock, my strength. As I go through this day, I will pause and think about all you have done for me. Like Hannah, I will rejoice and triumph in You Lord. I will remember there is no one as holy as You, there is none besides You. You are the one, true God in whom I depend on. I offer this prayer in worship and praise in Jesus' name today.

Song Suggestion: There is No Rock *by* Redeemer Music

Praise

Though the fig tree does not blossom and there is no fruit on the vines, [though] the product of the olive fails and the fields yield no food, though the flock is cut off from the fold and there are no cattle in the stalls, yet I will rejoice in the Lord; I will exult in the [victorious] God of my salvation!

Habakkuk 3:17-18 (Amp)

Father God,

Even though I am Your child, even though I try to live for You, even though I belong to You, there are always problems, disappointments, anxieties, and losses in my life. Even though there are so many things wrong, I know I can turn to You every minute of the day and You are there. As I seek Your Presence, You hold my hand. You give me strength, patience, and even joy. Yes, joy as I close my eyes and rest in Your arms. You will help me get through all my troubles. I trust You even though I do not know what is going to happen. As I lean on You now, hear my prayer of thanksgiving and praise. I praise You in the good times and in the bad. I praise You no matter the circumstances. I praise You because you are worthy of praise. Always. I pray this prayer of praise and thanksgiving in Jesus' name.

Song Suggestion: Praise You In This Storm *by* Casting Crowns

October 3

Wisdom

Happy (blessed, fortunate, enviable) is the man who finds skillful and godly Wisdom, and the man who gets understanding [drawing it forth from God's Word and life's experiences], for the gaining of it is better than the gaining of silver, and the profit of it better than fine gold.

Proverbs 3:13-14 (Amp)

God My Father,

How contrary Your Word is to the world in which I live. Accumulating money, status, and "stuff" seems to be what life is all about. The idea that the more we have, the happier we will be is the philosophy of our culture. Yet, You tell us that when we seek and find Your wisdom, we will be genuinely happy, and our life will be better than if we had more 'gold & silver.' I know this to be true on some level but there is always the quest for 'more' in my life. I thank You that Your Word teaches me what I need to be truly happy. I thank You for teaching me and opening my mind and heart to understand Your ways. Without Your revelation, I cannot grasp Your teachings and I am lost. I ask that you continue to increase my godly wisdom, continue to further my personal experiences with You, and continue to nurture my passion to be with You. I thank You, thank You that You hear me, and I believe You will answer me. I pray with deeply felt praise in Jesus' name today.

Song Suggestion: Blessings *by* Laura Story

October 4

Forgiven

[The Father] has delivered and drawn us to Himself out of the control and the dominion of darkness and has transferred us into the kingdom of the Son of His love, in Whom we have our redemption through His blood, [which means] the forgiveness of our sins.

Colossians 1:13-14 (Amp)

Father God,

You have rescued me. You have taken me out of darkness and put me into the kingdom of Your Son where I am surrounded in love. I do not always feel this way - but I have faith in Your Word. You have sent Jesus to rescue me, and I believe that through my belief in Jesus, I am redeemed and forgiven. I take this moment to declare my faith in You, to focus on the fact that I am forgiven, and to know I can live in Your kingdom forever. I can depend on You while I am living this life. I can think and meditate on the peace and joy that this faith gives. I am forgiven because of You. Let my praise and thanksgiving rise to You now. I pray in Jesus' saving name.

Song Suggestion: Love Ran Red *by* Chris Tomlin

Open Ears

Your righteous testimonies are everlasting and Your decrees are binding to eternity; give me understanding and I shall live [give me discernment and comprehension and I shall not die]. I cried with my whole heart; hear me, O Lord; I will keep Your statutes [I will hear, receive, love, and obey them].

Psalm 119:144-145 (Amp)

Father God,

Today I pray for a teachable heart. I humble myself before You, acknowledging that Your ways are the right ways, the best ways. I am in desperate need of You. I am desperate to hear from You. I pray this prayer right out of the psalm today: Please give me understanding, discernment, and comprehension of Your Word. I ask You to open my ears so that I will hear and receive Your teachings. I will love and obey them. Help me to surrender to You. I ask these things in the name of Jesus' today.

Song Suggestion: Word of God Speak *by* MercyMe

October 6

Joy

I lie awake thinking of you, meditating on you through the night. Because you are my helper, I sing for joy in the shadow of your wings.

Psalm 63:6-7 (NLT)

Father God,

I thank You that I am living in the shadow of your wings where I am always protected. Thank You for being my protector. I believe You are protecting me and my family. How many times have You helped me avoid a problem or a harmful situation? I am sure it is more than I will ever realize. I am sincerely grateful. Thank You for Your provision, Your protection, Your amazing love that You have for me. I choose to sing to You with joy when things are going great. I choose to sing to You with joy when things do not go my way. That is when I can run to You and sit quietly with You in the shadow of Your wings. Today I choose to live in Your joy. I pray this prayer with praise to You in Jesus' name.

Song Suggestion: Joy of the Lord *by* Rend Collective

Love God, Love Others

Owe nothing to anyone except to love one another; for the one who loves his neighbor has fulfilled the Law.

Romans 13:8 (NASB)

Father God,

You are my Father to whom I owe everything. You have given me my life, my breath, my family, my loved ones. You have also given me a chance to live my life with You. It is Your will that I love others and seek the best for them. Help me live my life this way.

Empower me to purposefully make choices that show Your love to others. Open my eyes to see opportunities where I can help other people. In these ways, I can honor, serve, and show my love to You every day. I praise You and I thank You for all the abilities that You have given me to accomplish Your wishes. I pray in gratitude in Jesus' name today.

Song Suggestion: Dream Small *by* Josh Wilson

October 8

Names of God

Abba

The defining term for 'Father' in the Aramaic Language; It is found in the New Testament only three times and is used only by Jesus and the apostle Paul.

And because you [really] are [His] sons, God has sent the [Holy] Spirit of His Son into our hearts, crying Abba (Father)! Father!

Galatians 4:6 (Amp)

Father God,

I thank You this morning for adopting me into Your family. You have called me Your son/daughter and sent Your Holy Spirit to live in me. You have become my Father whom I can come to, and You open Your arms for me. Jesus called You 'Abba' and I call You 'Abba' as well, my Father who I cherish and obey. I am filled with love, gratitude, and praise. I love to close my eyes in this moment and sit in Your holy, perfect Presence and breathe in Your peace and all that You are. You renew my spirit, and You revive my soul. It is You who gives me the strength I need to do Your will every day. Right now, I am calm, spending quiet time with You, my Father, declaring that You are holy, You are worthy and I am eternally grateful for such a perfect Abba, Father. In Jesus' name I pray all these things.

Song Suggestion: Live Up To Your Name *by* Danny Gokey

Jesus

And He has on His robe and on His thigh a name written: KING OF KINGS AND LORD OF LORDS.

Revelation 19:16 (NKJV)

Jesus,

You are the Lord of lords and the King of kings, and I worship You this morning. I thank You and I praise You. I am bowing now before you. I am nothing without You and I can do nothing without You. Thank you that not only are You my King, but You have also said that You are my friend. It is hard to wrap my mind around how holy, how powerful, how mighty You are yet You still consider me as someone whom You would think of. I am so thankful that You are reigning now and will continue to reign forever; I will be worshiping and praising You for all eternity. I close my eyes and see You dazzling in all Your glory. I pray in Your holy, powerful name this morning.

Song Suggestion: Agnus Dei - Holy You Are Holy Medley *by* Third Day

October 10

Eternity Minded

And He said to them, I say to you truly, there is no one who has left house or wife or brothers or parents or children for the sake of the kingdom of God who will not receive in return many times more in this world and, in the coming age, eternal life.

Luke 18:29-30 (Amp)

Father God,

You are a God Who rewards. I am Your child who likes to be rewarded! Help me to live more for You. Guide me in my actions to bring Your kingdom to my tiny part of the world. Give me the vision to see what I can do specifically for You. Grant me wisdom and discernment to know exactly what to do. Help me to be brave and courageous to follow Your path even though it may be difficult or unpopular. I will intentionally live each day with eternity in mind. Oh, I need lots of Your help! I put my hands out to You, Lord, so that You can guide me. In Jesus' name I pray.

Song Suggestion: Come Jesus Come *by* Stephen Mcwhirter

Believing

But these are written so that you may continue to believe that Jesus is the Messiah, the Son of God, and that by believing in him you will have life by the power of his name.

John 20:31 (NLT)

Father God,

I believe in Your holy Word that Jesus is the Messiah, Your Son. I believe because I have confidence in Him, I will have life, a spiritually full life here during my lifetime on earth and a full life in heaven for eternity. I am so thankful for God's plan and Jesus' work on the cross. I am so thankful for this gift of redemption from You, a gift I cannot purchase or earn myself. I bow down this morning before You to thank You, to praise You, to worship You for all You are and all You have done. I owe my life (earthly and eternal) to You Father, to You Jesus, and to You Holy Spirit. I pray with deep gratitude and love in Jesus' life-giving name.

Song Suggestion: I Believe It (The Life of Jesus) *by* Jon Reddick

October 12

Peace

You will guard him and keep him in perfect and constant peace whose mind [both its inclination and its character] is stayed on You, because he commits himself to You, leans on You and hopes confidently in You.

Isaiah 26:3 (Amp)

Father God,

Thank You for watching over me. Thank You for being so involved in my life. Thank You for giving me constant peace as I keep my mind on You. I commit myself to You as I lean on and hope confidently in You. As I learn to trust with more consistency and rely on You continually, Your peace will dwell in me. I am asking for Your help to guide my thoughts when they become agitated, fearful, offended. Let Your Holy Spirit override my thinking so that I am filled with Your serenity, Your tranquility. I need You and Your gentle persuasion to keep me connected to You. It is in You that I find all that I need. I am filled with gratitude and praise for Your perfect and constant peace that You make available to me. In Jesus' name I pray.

Song Suggestion: Find My Peace *by* Naomi Raine

October 13

God's Will

Show me Your ways, O LORD; Teach me Your paths, lead me in Your truth and teach me, for You are the God of my salvation; on You I wait all the day.

Psalm 24:4-5 (NKJV)

Father God,

Thank You for being a patient teacher and guide. Thank You for being the one, true God, the God Who saves me. I pray this psalm to You this morning. I want to know Your will for me. I want to walk on Your path. I want to carry out Your plans. I want to know and live in Your truth. Help me, guide me, Lord. You know how I desperately need You. I will sit in Your Presence this morning waiting expectantly. Being quiet with You in the morning gets me ready to face the day's challenges knowing that You are with me. I am giving You thanks in advance for helping me know, understand, and carry out Your will. I pray this prayer in Jesus' saving name.

Song Suggestion: Lead Me *by* Sanctus Real

October 14

Thoughts/Mindset

Don't copy the behavior and customs of this world, but let God transform you into a new person by changing the way you think. Then you will learn to know God's will for you, which is good and pleasing and perfect. Because of the privilege and authority God has given me, I give each of you this warning: Don't think you are better than you really are. Be honest in your evaluation of yourselves, measuring yourselves by the faith God has given us.

Romans 12:2-3 (NLT)

Father God,

Thank You for Your truth which has been written down for all to read. Thank You that You are the One, the only One, who can transform me into the person I was created to be. Help me to allow You to change my thinking, my mindset, my attitudes. Guide me to see Your truth rather than what the culture tells me is true. The world has an abundance of lies, deceptions, disinformation - it is extremely difficult to know what is real, what is true. It is so easy to think that I am always right. But Your Word cautions me to make sure I measure my own thoughts based on my faith in You. I am left with only one solution. I humble myself and surrender to You. I put myself in Your hands like I am doing in this moment and pray You will help me with my thought life. I am trusting and hoping in You.

I believe knowing Your truth and Your love will change me. I pray for all these things, grateful that I can come to You, in Jesus' name.

Song Suggestion: The Change in Me *by* Casting Crowns

October 15

The Presence of God

HE WHO dwells in the secret place of the Most High shall remain stable and fixed under the shadow of the Almighty [Whose power no foe can withstand]. I will say of the Lord, He is my Refuge and my Fortress, my God; on Him I lean and rely, and in Him I [confidently] trust!

Psalm 91:1-2 (Amp)

Father God,

You are the Most High, You are the almighty God, having complete, awesome power over all things. I am putting myself in Your secret place where I can remain stable and content. I am relying on Your daily training to strengthen my dedication to living in Your holy Presence. My intentions are good and true but my follow through is often weak. I ask the Holy Spirit to constantly remind me (loudly, aggressively, repeatedly) to meditate on all You are and all You are doing for me throughout each day. Remind me that You are to be praised and worshiped. Remind me that I can bring You all my thoughts, problems, observations, and fears to You all day long. Remind me that I can include You in my life every hour of every day. I want to live, dwell, and remain in Your Presence.

You are my peace, my refuge, my fortress. I can lean on You, I can rely on You and in You I can trust, every day! I pray with gratitude for Your Presence in my life in Jesus' name.

Song Suggestion: Secret Place *by* Hillsong Worship

Trust God

For we walk by faith [we regulate our lives and conduct ourselves by our conviction or belief respecting man's relationship to God and divine things, with trust and holy fervor; thus we walk] not by sight or appearance.

2 Corinthians 5:7 (Amp)

Father God,

Thank You that I can be honest with You and declare that I have so many weaknesses and doubts. Sometimes I wonder if I can put my total trust in You and relinquish all control. Your Word says that I can. You promise to be with me, help and strengthen me. I believe that You will take my hand. Right now, I am stepping out in faith, and I am putting my hand in Yours. I am submitting to You my fears and anxieties. (**Note**: *Communicate to God what is on your mind.*) I will ask You what to do and I will obey You and I will let You do the rest. I will let You do what I cannot do. I will surrender my life and put myself in Your hands. I will wait and thank You while I am waiting. I will get up each day trusting You are working things out on my behalf. I am thanking You right now that I can trust You. I am praising You right now because I can walk by faith with Your help. I pray in Jesus' trustworthy name today.

Song Suggestion: Walk By Faith *by* Jeremy Camp

October 17

Forgiving

And forgive us our sins, for we also forgive everyone who is indebted to us. And do not lead us into temptation, but deliver us from the evil one."

Luke 11:4 (NKJV)

Jesus,

In Your words, You have taught us to ask You for forgiveness but You also tell us to forgive others no matter what. I admit that I often do not want to, or I do not "feel like" forgiving others. I admit that I sometimes hold grudges and/or hold onto my anger.

Today I declare to You Lord, that I am sorry for not choosing to forgive quickly and easily as You have taught. I ask You to help me learn to live like You - extending grace and mercy to others whether they deserve it or not. I am choosing to forgive others. I am choosing to overlook offenses. I am choosing to be kind and merciful when people are rude or disagreeable with me. I want to live this way and I ask for Your help. I thank You and praise You for the forgiveness that You have shown me. I thank You and praise You for the help that You will give me to forgive others. I pray all these things in Jesus' compassionate name.

Song Suggestion: The Lord's Prayer *by* Hillsong Worship

October 18

My Words

Now when the people complained, it displeased the LORD; for the LORD heard it, and His anger was aroused. So the fire of the LORD burned among them, and consumed some in the outskirts of the camp.

Numbers 11:1 (NKJV)

Father God,

I sit quietly with You this morning thinking about how You can hear every single thing I say. I admit that I say many things that offend You. I complain when I don't get my own way, when I disagree with others around me, or when life gets difficult. I complain about the gifts that You have given me (family, work, house, car, spouse) when I should be thanking You for these things. I want to please You, not kindle Your anger. I am learning that my complaining and whining is not Your will for me. I have decided that I am going to work on eliminating my complaints until they are no longer a part of who I am. With Your help, I will turn my complaining into thanksgiving. I ask You to give me the wisdom and perseverance to change. I believe that I can break this sinful habit that I have of complaining and that I can shine as Your light instead. Thank You for Your instruction.

Thank You for working with me. Thank You for having mercy on me when I falter. I know that You are kind and compassionate to me. In Jesus' patient name I pray today.

Song Suggestion: Count My Blessings *by* Seph Schlueter

October 19

Anxiety

So humble yourselves under the mighty power of God, and at the right time he will lift you up in honor. Give all your worries and cares to God, for he cares about you.

1 Peter 5:6-7 (NLT)

Father God,

I humbly come before You, admitting that I cannot fix all my own life's circumstances. I cannot control the chaos, the problems, and the stressors in my life. I have tried to do this all on my own and it has left me overwhelmed and defeated. I know I cannot live my life on my own. I need You. I need You to lean on. I am casting my cares upon You this morning. Specifically, I have been struggling with… (**Note**: *Communicate to God what is on your mind*). I will listen to see if there is anything You would like me to do. Then I am giving these cares to You completely and I am letting them go. I am waiting for You to step in. I am thanking You for working on my behalf while I wait. Instead of worrying and talking about my problems over and over again, I will praise and thank You instead for Your goodness, Your promises, and Your blessings. I believe You are working in my life even if I cannot see or feel it! I am full of relief and gratitude that I can give You my worries and cares because You care deeply for me. I pray all these things in Jesus' name today.

Song Suggestion: On Repeat *by* Hillsong United

October 20

Thankful

Oh, give thanks to the Lord! Call upon His name; make known His deeds among the peoples!

12 Remember His marvelous works which He has done, His wonders, and the judgments of His mouth,

1 Chronicles 16:8,12 (NKJV)

Father God,

I come to You every morning with thanksgiving in my heart and on my lips. I am grateful that You hear my prayers. You open the door and I enter into Your Presence when I call Your name. You have done marvelous works in my life. You have forgiven me. You have opened Your arms and let me run to You over and over. Your mercy and compassion never fail me. You have adopted me as Your child. These are just some of Your blessings which I am grateful for. I sit in Your holy Presence now and I let my thankfulness flow from my heart to Yours. I grab hold of all the wonders of Your love, and I hold them close to my heart. I am thankful now and I will be thankful always. In Jesus' name I pray today.

Song Suggestion: Grateful *by* Elevation Worship

Prayer

Be earnest and unwearied and steadfast in your prayer [life], being [both] alert and intent in [your praying] with thanksgiving.

Colossians 4:2 (Amp)

Father God,

Oh, that I would be devoted to prayer as the apostle Paul has instructed. I do love our prayer time where we spend this time together each day. Help me to be more consistent, persistent, steadfast, and dedicated to You. You are worthy of being praised, honored, worshiped, and glorified each day. I am so thankful that You also want a relationship with me, a personal and intimate relationship. I will take time now to tell You what is on my mind today. (**Note**: *Communicate to God some things that are going on in your life, others' lives, and/or your personal thoughts to share.*) I thank You for being such a good Father who listens, who loves, who cares about everything in my life. I love coming to You in prayer each day. I pray in Jesus' name today.

Song Suggestion: Don't Stop Praying *by* Matthew West

Seek God

And it is impossible to please God without faith. Anyone who wants to come to him must believe that God exists and that he rewards those who sincerely seek him.

Hebrews 11:6 (NLT)

Father God,

I am here this morning, and it is You I seek! You are the ONE who gives me salvation. It is You Who gives me an abundant and eternal life starting the moment I believed in You, the moment I put my hope, faith, and trust in You. I believe You are rewarding me every day. When good things happen, I have faith that it is You working in my life, it is not just coincidence. I am thankful for all Your favor and blessings in my life. Open my eyes so I am aware of the favor and blessings You give me. I will intentionally seek You every day. I am so thankful that You can be found! I pray this prayer in Jesus' holy name today.

Song Suggestion: Open Up the Heavens *by* Vertical Worship

Discouragement

Blessed be the God and Father of our Lord Jesus Christ, the Father of mercies and God of all comfort, who comforts us in all our tribulation, that we may be able to comfort those who are in any trouble, with the comfort with which we ourselves are comforted by God.

2 Corinthians 1:3-4 (NKJV)

Father God,

I thank You for being my comforter. I sit in this quiet place and rest wholly and totally in You. Although I have feelings of discouragement and disappointment in my life, I have faith that You can give me rest. In You, I find comfort and peace. I take the time this morning to just breathe, rest, breathe, rest, in Your holy, peaceful Presence. I let Your peace and Your strength envelop me and fill me. I thank You for Your comfort. I praise You for Your strength. Help me to live my life using my words and actions to encourage and comfort others as You comfort me. I pray these things with praise and gratitude in Jesus' merciful name.

Song Suggestion: Run to the Father *by* Cody Carnes

God's Love

But you, O Lord, are a God of compassion and mercy, slow to get angry and filled with unfailing love and faithfulness.

Psalm 86:15 (NLT)

Father God,

Today I am leaning into Your love. I am shutting out the world's confusion and noise. I am focusing my thoughts on You and Your unfailing love and faithfulness to me. I am running into Your arms and allowing You to saturate my spirit, my heart, and my soul with Your radiant light, love, joy, peace, compassion, and mercy. I am safe with You. As I experience complete contentment, I send forth my love, my praise, my awe, my deep gratitude to You. That is all I have to give. I love You; I praise You; I thank You Father, Spirit, and Jesus. I pray in Jesus' compassionate name today.

Song Suggestion: How You Love Me *by* Patrick Mayberry

October 25

Hope

For in Him does our heart rejoice, because we have trusted (relied on and been confident) in His holy name. Let Your mercy and loving-kindness, O Lord, be upon us, in proportion to our waiting and hoping for You.

Psalm 33:21-22 (Amp)

Father God,

Today I have decided that I will trust You wholeheartedly. I am giving You my concerns, my worries, my schedule. I am letting go of it all and I am choosing hope, peace, and joy as I am trusting You to 'make my paths straight' and help me navigate my life's journey Your way. As I wait and hope in You with more consistency, I will see Your loving kindness and mercy in my life. Oh, what a better life I will have as I live with an expectancy of hope with You at my side. I am humbled, grateful, and full of praise for You, my hope. You are the hope of the world. I pray in Jesus' trustworthy name.

Song Suggestion: Overcome *by* Elevation Worship

October 26

Perseverance

But as for you, be strong and courageous, for your work will be rewarded.

2 Chronicles 15:7 (NLT)

Father God,

Today I am praying for strength. Because You are with me and helping me, I believe I am strong. I pray for determination that will not diminish when I'm faced with adversity or difficulty. I pray for courage that will increase in the face of my fears. I pray for perseverance when I am tired, overwhelmed, and feel ready to give up. You have said that there will be troubles in my life. Even though life gets difficult and at times there are challenges that seem insurmountable, I will remember that You are with me, You will not leave me. I will run to You. I will place my obstacles in Your care, and You will help me carry them as I lean on You. I will be strong and courageous. I will press on, praising You and thanking You through it all. I look forward to the day when I will be rewarded by You. I pray these things in Jesus' victorious name.

Song Suggestion: Strong *by* Anne Wilson

I am a Child of God

Now you are no longer a slave but God's own child. And since you are his child, God has made you his heir.

Galatians 4:7 (NLT)

Father God,

I am meditating this morning on Your amazing mercy and love that has allowed me to become Your child, a child of the Almighty, all powerful, omniscient God. I am an heir - I have been given the privilege to live in Your kingdom - starting now! I can call on You all day long. I can rely on You and trust that Your promises to me are true. You have promised to never leave me, to save me (give me salvation), to be faithful to me (even when I am not faithful to You), to give me a purpose, to allow me to be in Your Presence, to strengthen me and give me wisdom as well as an abundant life. All these promises bring me peace, joy, and hope. Your promises are good because You are a good Father, full of kindness, compassion, faithfulness, and love. I am so thankful and give You praise for all You are! I am so thankful and give You praise for who You have made me to be - Your child. I pray with deep and profound praise and gratitude in Jesus' name today.

Song Suggestion: No Longer Slaves *by* Bethel Music

October 28

Motivation

How shall a young man cleanse his way? By taking heed and keeping watch [on himself] according to Your word [conforming his life to it].

15 I will meditate on Your precepts and have respect to Your ways [the path of life marked out by Your law].

Psalm 119:9,15 (Amp)

Father God,

Thank You for giving me a guide that shows me Your way. I ask You to come into my heart and my mind and to ignite a passion - an internal, fiery, persistent motivation in me - to read, study, and meditate on Your Word. I want my life to be aligned with You and Your ways. As I grow closer to You and learn from You, my path will open up before me and You will be with me on that path. I am thankful for this blessing, this gift. I am thankful that You have given me direction so I can know Your precepts and Your ways. I praise You in Jesus' name today.

Song Suggestion: The Heart of Worship *by* Matt Redman

Pray for Others

Pray at all times (on every occasion, in every season) in the Spirit, with all [manner of] prayer and entreaty. To that end keep alert and watch with strong purpose and perseverance interceding in behalf of all saints (God's consecrated people).

Ephesians 6:18 (Amp)

Heavenly Father,

I believe You hear my prayers. You tell me to pray at all times and so I am thankful that I can come to You repeatedly and bring everything that is on my mind to You. I thank You that You are working in my life. You also tell me to intercede on behalf of all Your people. I pray for all Your believers as well as my family and friends. I pray that we will experience and be made aware of how good, kind, and merciful You are. I pray that we will feel Your peace in our lives more consistently. I pray that we will learn to trust You and live more fully in Your Presence. I pray specific requests for those around me. (**Note**: *Communicate to God anyone that you know who has needs.*) I raise my prayers of requests mixed with prayers of praise, thanksgiving, and worship to You my Father, to Jesus, my Savior, and to the Holy Spirit. In Jesus' name I pray these prayers today.

Song Suggestion: When We Pray *by* Tauren Wells

I am… the Body of Christ

Now you [collectively] are Christ's body and [individually] you are members of it, each part severally and distinct [each with his own place and function].

1 Corinthians 12:27 (Amp)

Father God,

The apostle Paul says that I am the body of Christ. My first thought is that I am not worthy, and I think of all that I am not. However, as I sit in Your Presence in this moment, I know that You are changing me ever so slowly. Help me internalize Your teachings and do my best to live in such a way that honors You in my daily life. Challenge me to be committed to do all I can to learn Your ways. Help me to be convinced of the things I need to change and help me to work with You to change them and not reason my way out of it. I pray that again, Lord: Let Your Holy Spirit convince me of the things I need to change and help me to cooperate rather than talk myself out of it. You are reminding me right now that I am the body of Christ. Other people are watching me (even if I don't realize it). So, I ask You to help me. Holy Spirit, grab my hand and my heart and pull me along Your prepared path. Help me to honor You and represent You well along the way. I ask all these things with great hope and expectation in Jesus' name.

Song Suggestion: The Cause of Christ *by* Kari Jobe

I Will...

DO NOT judge and criticize and condemn others, so that you may not be judged and criticized and condemned yourselves. For just as you judge and criticize and condemn others, you will be judged and criticized and condemned, and in accordance with the measure you [use to] deal out to others, it will be dealt out again to you.

Matthew 7:1-2 (Amp)

Father God,

After reading this scripture where Jesus is teaching, I am thoroughly and deeply convicted because, at times, I am quick to judge, quick to criticize and quick to condemn others. It comes easily and naturally to me because I think I am always right! Therefore, I am left to humbly bow at Your feet and ask first for Your forgiveness. I am sorry that I often think too highly of my own opinions and beliefs, and I disregard others' as inferior or wrong. I am sorry that I have a critical spirit and I think my way is the best way. I am sorry for looking down on others for so many reasons that I cannot even itemize them. I am sorry and I would like to change this critical, condescending, and judgmental attitude that I have. I ask You to burrow into my mind and my heart and begin to mold me to be more like Jesus. Help me to think first of mercy and grace. Help me to think first of compassion and love. Let these thoughts overtake all others. I will have an accepting attitude. I will be merciful. I will be quick to listen and slow to judge, criticize, and condemn. I will give people the benefit of the doubt. I will give people a break. I will try to understand that others have lots of negative situations in their lives that cause them to act in a different way than me. I will shine Your light over the darkness in our world rather than contribute to it. Help me Holy Spirit every single day. In Jesus' merciful name I pray.

Song Suggestion: Relate *by* for King and Country

Holy Sovereign God

Ascribe to the Lord the glory due His name. Bring an offering and come before Him; worship the Lord in the beauty of holiness and in holy array. Tremble and reverently fear before Him, all the earth's peoples; the world also shall be established, so it cannot be moved. Let the heavens be glad and let the earth rejoice; and let men say among the nations, The Lord reigns!

1 Chronicles 16:29-31 (Amp)

Father God,

I love this time that we share together. This is the most important part of my day. I am focusing on You and building a relationship with the one, true God who loves me, the One who created me. I bring an offering of myself today. I want to worship You in the beauty of Your holiness. I want to praise You and give You honor and glory, not just in this minute but all through my day. I am joining the heavens and rejoicing that You are on Your throne; You are in charge. You reign over us all. You are the holy Lord and I want to live with You and for You today and every day. I pray all these things in Jesus' holy name.

Song Suggestion: Reign Above It All *by* Bethel Music feat Paul McClure

November 2

Praise

Bless the LORD, O my soul; and all that is within me, bless His holy name! Bless the LORD, O my soul, and forget not all His benefits; Who forgives all your iniquities, Who heals all your diseases, Who redeems your life from destruction, Who crowns you with lovingkindness and tender mercies,

Psalm 103:1-4 (NKJV)

Father God,

When I read this psalm, I think about all You have done for me. You have forgiven me so many times. You heal me again and again. You have redeemed me from a life of destruction by sending Jesus to pay the price that I should have paid. You care for me by covering me with Your loving kindness and mercy. For these reasons and countless more, I am sending my love and gratitude from deep inside me to You, my Father, my Jesus, my Lord. I am blessing You with all that is within me. I am willfully centering my life around You. I am conscientiously thinking about all You do for me every day. I am living my life in a way to honor and praise You. I praise You and glorify You today and all my days. I pray this prayer in Jesus' holy name.

Song Suggestion: 10,000 Reasons (Bless the Lord) *by* Matt Redman

November 3

Wisdom

Hear counsel, receive instruction, and accept correction, that you may be wise in the time to come. Many plans are in a man's mind, but it is the Lord's purpose for him that will stand.

Proverbs 19:20-21 (Amp)

Father God,

I am here this morning to spend time and connect with You. I am here this morning to be molded by You. I humbly come before You as someone who needs Your help in getting me on track and keeping me there. I need Your vision and input to help me participate in Your plan for me. I thank You that You have plans for me; Your plans are good. I give You my empty hands. I trust that You are working in my life. I cannot wait to see what will happen as I learn and as I follow You as best as I can. Help me hear Your counsel. Help me to receive Your instruction with an open mind and accommodating attitude.

Help me to accept Your correction. Guide me to have the mind of Christ. I am so thankful for the work You are doing in my life. I pray with deep gratitude, and I ask every one of these things in Jesus' name.

Song Suggestion: Tend *by* Emmy Rose, Bethel Music

Forgiven

For I will be merciful and gracious toward their sins and I will remember their deeds of unrighteousness no more.

Hebrews 8:12 (Amp)

Father God,

This morning, I sit quietly removing all distractions from my mind. I think about Your abundant, overflowing, and continual mercy and grace toward me. I am truly humbled by Your deep love and care that is poured on me as I worship and praise You. Your Word declares that You will 'remember deeds of unrighteousness no more.' I wonder how this can be, especially because I often make the same mistakes repeatedly. I often leave You to go off and do my own thing with no thought of You. This morning, I say again, I am sorry for my sins, and I accept, by faith, Your forgiveness. I ask You to continue to help me live a life worthy of the loving kindness and compassion that You continually give. I meditate on Your mercy and grace and the love and peace that it gives me as I start this day with You. My love and gratitude flows to You in this moment because I am forgiven. In Jesus' name I gratefully pray.

Song Suggestion: Forgiven *by* David Crowder

November 5

Open Ears

So pay attention to how you hear. To those who listen to my teaching, more understanding will be given. But for those who are not listening, even what they think they understand will be taken away from them."

Luke 8:18 (NLT)

Father God,

I admit that there are so many things that I do not understand about You and Your ways as they seem opposite of what the culture I live in dictates. I am sure there are many areas where I think I have the "right" idea, but I am probably off the mark. I come humbly to You asking You to help me hear. Guide me to listen to Your teachings. Then help me to apply the teaching to my own life. Open my eyes and ears to Your truth. I need Your guidance always. I will not give up trying to hear You, as long as You do not give up trying to teach me. Thank You for Your patience and Your love. Let me be a person who listens. Let me be that person whose light grows brighter and brighter, reflecting images of You. In Jesus' name I pray this prayer.

Song Suggestion: Voice of Truth *by* Casting Crowns

November 6

Joy

And Nehemiah, who was the governor, Ezra the priest and scribe, and the Levites who taught the people said to all the people, "This day is holy to the LORD your God; do not mourn nor weep." For all the people wept when they heard the words of the Law. Then he said to them, "Go your way, eat the fat, drink the sweet, and send portions to those for whom nothing is prepared for this day is holy to our Lord. Do not sorrow, for the joy of the LORD is your strength."

Nehemiah 8:9-10 (NKJV)

Father God,

When I read this scripture, I am overcome by how much You love Your people, how much You care for us. You remind me to care for others as well. You do not want me to be burdened or overwhelmed. You want me to live a life that is joyful, dependent upon You. You are my strength. You will help me and take care of me. It is OK that I rest in You. It is OK that I enjoy the blessings that You have given me. It is OK that I take some time to slow the pace of this life I am living. I take this moment right now to let these thoughts soak into my mind. I let Your strength fill me in this moment. I let Your joy fill me. I just breathe. As I enter into this day, I ask You to remind me that You are with me, You are helping me. The joy of You Lord, is my strength. I pray this prayer with gratitude in Jesus' name.

Song Suggestion: Joy of the Lord *by* Mac Powell

November 7

Love God/Love Others

Dear friends, let us continue to love one another, for love comes from God. Anyone who loves is a child of God and knows God. But anyone who does not love does not know God, for God is love.

1 John 4:7-8 (NLT)

Father God,

Thank You for showing me Your love persistently and continually in so many ways. Thank You for increasing my awareness of Your love for me to a greater degree. Your love is the foundation of my faith, and I am so grateful that my faith in You is deepening. You are love. You are pure. You are worthy. I should praise You and thank You many times over. As You make me more aware of Your love, I pray that You will continue to awaken in me a love for others. I ask the Holy Spirit to point out someone whom I can show God's love to today. Give me the courage to follow through. Let me be a person who lives everyday spreading Your love, kindness, and generosity to everyone around me. I pray these things in Jesus' loving name.

Song Suggestion: Follow You *by* Leeland

Names of God

Jehovah Shammah

In Hebrew this means 'The Lord is there' and is the name given to the city in Ezekial's vision.

The distance around the city shall by 18,000 [4 x 4,500] measures; and the name of the city from that day and ever after shall be, THE LORD IS THERE.

Ezekiel 48:35 (Amp)

Father God,

Thank You that You are a God who plans. You have laid the foundation of the world and what is to come. Your plans will not fail. Thank You that You will be forever with Your people. Thank You that You have shared glimpses of what is to come. I am putting my faith in You and on that day in the future where 'You will be there.' You will be in a place where You are at the center. In a place that has been made new. In a place where there is only light and goodness. In a place where there is only peace and joy. I am making my plan as well. I am planning on being there with You. I will be forever praising You, worshiping You, and thanking You. You are worthy of all the glory and praise. I pray this prayer in Jesus' victorious name.

Song Suggestion: Is He Worthy *by* Chris Tomlin

Jesus

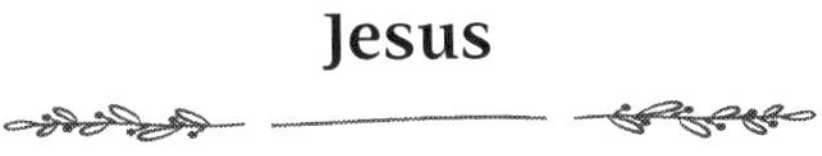

I am the Good Shepherd. The Good Shepherd risks and lays down His [own] life for the sheep.

John 10:11 (Amp)

Jesus,

I need You. I need a shepherd. Thank You for watching over me day and night. Thank You for putting Your protective arms around me. Thank You for leading me to what is best. I trust You. I seek You and I declare that I want to follow You right now and every day. As I do my best to follow You, I am grateful for Your unending goodness and kindness. How can I ever show You my gratitude? You laid down Your life. Willingly. And for me. I thank You and I praise You again and again. I am in awe of all You have done. I put up my empty hands and say to You, my Shepherd, "Here I am ... help me to follow you." I am praying in deep gratitude in Jesus' name today.

Song Suggestion: Shepherd *by* Amanda Cook

November 10

Eternity Minded

So you must remain faithful to what you have been taught from the beginning. If you do, you will remain in fellowship with the Son and with the Father. And in this fellowship we enjoy the eternal life he promised us.

1 John 2:24-25 (NLT)

My Father God,

I come to You with great awe of Your great power and Your amazing plans and promises. I pray this morning asking You to help me remain faithful and consistent in my discipleship to You. Guide me as I strive to know You better. This is my plea every day, every week, of every month, year upon year. May I trust and abide in You until I gain the promise of eternal life. I praise You and thank You for making a way for me to be with You forever. Forever in Your light. Forever in Your warmth. Forever in Your love. Forever in Your Presence. What a wondrous day that will be. I pray in Jesus,' my Savior's name today.

Song Suggestion: Glorious Day (Living He Loved Me) *by* Casting Crowns

Believing

For I am not ashamed of the gospel of Christ, for it is the power of God to salvation for everyone who believes, for the Jew first and also for the Greek.

Romans 1:16 (NKJV)

Father God,

It is getting harder and harder to stand up for You in the world I live in. To do so may set me apart from those around me and many will look suspiciously at me. Even so, I am declaring to You right now that I believe in You, My God and Father. I believe in You, Jesus, Son of God, my Savior. I believe in You, the Holy Spirit given to me. I believe our relationship is growing and evolving. I believe I am as close to You as I choose. I pray that You will help me get more comfortable letting others know that I believe in You, that I belong to You. I am so grateful to have this faith. I am so grateful to You for Your good news - the gospel of Jesus. I pray in Jesus' holy name.

Song Suggestion: I Believe *by* Phil Wickham

Peace

If possible, as far as it depends on you, live at peace with everyone.

Romans 12:18 (Amp)

Father God,

I have asked You to guide me and show me Your ways repeatedly. Here in this moment, with this scripture, You have answered my prayer. Thank You for Your direct instruction that I can find in Your Word. Help me to enhance my ability to obey You and live in peace with everyone. Yes, everyone. I ask the Holy Spirit to bring this directive to my mind when I am dealing with unkind, agitating people, when I am in disagreement with others, when I am feeling angry, when I feel offended or disrespected, when I am driving in traffic, when my feelings are hurt, when I am at home with my spouse and my family. I need You in so many of these daily situations. Help me, help me to be peaceful inside and out. I cannot do this without Your help. I rely on You as I try to think, act, and react peaceably. Thank You for forgiving me and keeping a peaceful attitude toward me. You are the ultimate model of peace and I give You praise for demonstrating such peace. I pray in Jesus' peaceful name.

Song Suggestion: Let There Be Peace On Earth *by* Vince Gill

November 13

God's Will

He who deals wisely and heeds [God's word] and counsel shall find good, and whoever leans on, trusts in, and is confident in the Lord - happy, blessed, and fortunate is he.

Proverbs 16:20 (Amp)

God, my Father,

You are a God Who blesses me when I learn and live by Your Word and Your ways. You are a God Who is faithful and gives grace, mercy, and blessings to me because I trust in You. Thank You, Father, that Your will for me is to know You intimately and live for You joyfully. You are blessing me continually. Open my eyes to Your blessings. I will live in gratitude to You for Your favor that You shower on me. While I do not deserve all that You give, I still reach out my empty hands to receive Your counsel, grace, mercy, love, favor, and benefits. You are truly a good Father Who wants to reward me for heeding Your Word. I am so deeply grateful and will live gratefully as You give me confidence, happiness, and blessings as I lean on and trust in You as I do my best to do Your will. I pray for these things with praise and worship in Jesus' faithful name.

Song Suggestion: I'm Gonna Walk With Jesus *by* Consumed by Fire

Thoughts/Mindset

And whatever you do [no matter what it is] in word or deed, do everything in the name of the Lord Jesus and in [dependence upon] His Person, giving praise to God the Father through Him.

Colossians 3:17 (Amp)

Father God,

Thank You for the tasks You have for me today. I am choosing to set my mind on doing everything - big and little - for You today. When I go to work/school, I will do my best, working with integrity and excellence. I will work diligently for You, not for my supervisors, for personal praise or for my paycheck, but for You. When I am doing errands/chores, I will do them with a grateful attitude, thanking and praising You that I have the opportunity and ability to accomplish these activities. I believe by having this mindset, I will become closer to You. I am excited to start my day with You at my side. Help me, motivate me to be consistent and steadfast in developing this life changing mindset. Father, You are my strength and my joy today. Everything I do today, I will do it for You, Father, Spirit, and Jesus. I pray with praise to You in Jesus' name today.

Song Suggestion: Do Everything *by* Steven Curtis Chapman

November 15

The Presence of God

"Abide in Me, and I in you. As the branch cannot bear fruit of itself, unless it abides in the vine, neither can you, unless you abide in Me. "I am the vine, you are the branches. He who abides in Me, and I in him, bears much fruit; for without Me you can do nothing.

John 15:4-5 (NKJV)

Father God,

I take time this morning to sit in Your Presence and breathe in Your goodness. You reach out Your hand to me and You invite me to 'remain in You.' I know that I can do nothing worthwhile without You, and I am ever so slowly learning what it means to 'abide in You.' I ask You to encourage me as I attempt to stay in Your Presence by praising You, thanking You, and praying to You during our morning time and all through the day. I believe You are giving me grace and determination as I make slow progress. I open my heart and empty hands to thank You! Thank You for being my 'vine,' thank You for helping me abide in You and for abiding in me. Thank You for increasing my faith and leading me in the way I should go. I need You so very much. I pray all these things in Jesus' name.

Song Suggestion: Abide (Live at The Worship Initiative) *by* Aaron Williams

November 16

Trust God

Cause me to hear Your loving-kindness in the morning, for on You do I lean and in You do I trust. Cause me to know the way wherein I should walk for I lift up my inner self to You.

Psalm 143:8 (Amp)

Father God,

I am starting my day with the goal of allowing Your loving kindness to surround me in this moment and all throughout my day. You are my helper, my guide in this life and I need You every minute. I am putting my trust in You to help me and guide me. I need You to have a meaningful and worthy life. Penetrate my heart, my mind, and my soul with Your courage, Your fearlessness, Your power, Your boldness. Wherever You want me to go, whatever You want me to do, I believe You will give me the ability, the fortitude, the determination, and the power to do Your will. I trust You. I trust You along every step of our journey together. I pray in Jesus' victorious name.

Song Suggestion: Lions *by* Skillet

November 17

Forgiving

Hatred stirs up contentions, but love covers all transgressions.

Proverbs 10:12 (Amp)

Father God,

It is so easy for me to tell You how I will be forgiving and loving when I am here in Your Presence, where I can sense Your love, kindness, and forgiveness toward me. My intentions to forgive are pure and true. But when I leave this peaceful, tranquil prayer time and reenter the social world of other people, my good intentions are often left at home in my 'prayer chair.' That's when I need Your Holy Spirit to yell (loudly) in my ear and remind me of my intentions to forgive and show mercy to others. I genuinely want to bring You glory, obey You and live in Your love. I believe You will continue to work patiently with me. I believe I am improving even though I am not where I want to be. I thank You, thank You for Your Word and Your Holy Spirit which helps me forgive others as You forgive me. I need You, Lord. I pray in Jesus' merciful name today.

Song Suggestion: Make Room *by* Community Music

November 18

My Words

He who guards his mouth keeps his life, but he who opens wide his lips comes to ruin.

Proverbs 13:3 (Amp)

Holy, Father God,

I am learning from Your Word about how important it is for me to be careful about what I say so that I can please You and have a better life. Help me give praise and gratitude rather than complain. Help me to remember Your gifts and blessings rather than focus on circumstances that make me unhappy. Help me use my words to encourage, bless, and shower kindness on everyone I encounter. Help me think before I speak, especially when I am angry, hurt, disappointed, or frustrated. Oh, how I need Your help, Holy Spirit! I cannot do this in my own strength so I will continue to ask for Your help, as I continue to lean on You. Thank You for being my helper and my guide as I walk on this journey with You. I thank You and praise You as You are faithful and true. In Jesus' name I pray.

Song Suggestion: Your Words *by* Third Day

Anxiety

With this news, strengthen those who have tired hands, and encourage those who have weak knees. Say to those with fearful hearts, "Be strong, and do not fear, for your God is coming to destroy your enemies. He is coming to save you."

Isaiah 35:3-4 (NLT)

Father God,

Thank You for the times when things are going great in my life! Thank You for the times when things are not going my way, when I am full of anxieties and concerns. Thank You for being with me in both the easy, good times as well as the difficult, stressful times.

You stay the same even though I can be an emotional roller coaster! I believe You are with me, you are encouraging me. You are giving me strength and giving me courage when I need it. You are a God Who saves, and You have already saved me. I rely on these promises when anxiety fills me. I call on Your faithfulness and trustworthiness. As I do, I watch You catching me and wrapping me in light, in peace, in safety. I inhale Your tranquility and holiness. I hold these moments in my heart, and this helps me to carry on. Thank You I pray in Jesus' name.

Song Suggestion: Safe In Your Arms *by* Josh Baldwin feat kalley

November 20

Thankful

Oh, that men would give thanks to the LORD *for His goodness, and for His wonderful works to the children of men! For He satisfies the longing soul, and fills the hungry soul with goodness.*

Psalm 107:8-9 (NKJV)

Father God,

I am so thankful for ALL the blessings You have poured upon my life. Thank You for Your love and care that You shower over me daily. Thank You for the family that You have given me. Thank You for my home and for keeping me safe. Thank You for heat when it is cold, for clean water that I take for granted every day. Thank You for clean air to breathe! Thank You for the work You've given me to do, even though I often complain about it. Thank You for providing for my physical and spiritual needs. You satisfy my soul and consistently fill me with goodness. You are my loving Father Who blesses me more than I can ever know. Thank You, thank You, thank You. I pray in deep, heartfelt gratitude for all You have done and for all You have given in Jesus' name today.

Song Suggestion: Thank You *by* 33 Miles

Prayer

But in my distress I cried out to the LORD; yes, I prayed to my God for help. He heard me from his sanctuary; my cry to him reached his ears.

Psalm 18:6 (NLT)

Father God,

I am so thankful that You hear me. You listen to my cries for help. You listen to my prayers for others. You listen to my requests for peace, healing, joy, and protection. You listen when I am discouraged, and You listen when I am thankful and joyful. Sometimes I wonder how You can hear me when there is so much going on in the world. But You are a wondrous mystery. You are amazing and good. Today I pray for… (**Note**: *Communicate to God anything that comes to mind*). I lift my voice to You with gratitude and love because You are a God who listens, who hears, who cares for me. In Jesus' name I pray today.

Song Suggestion: God Who Listens *by* Chris Tomlin feat Thomas Rhett

November 22

Seek God

The L*ORD* *is good to those who wait for Him, to the soul who seeks Him. It is good that one should hope and wait quietly for the salvation of the* L*ORD.*

Lamentations 3:25-26 (NKJV)

God, my Father,

You have been so good to me. I am so very thankful for the many blessings in my life. I am thankful that I can seek You and sit quietly with You every day. I am thankful for every new season that You give me in my life. You are constantly changing me and watching me grow. I thank You for opening new doors for me, for giving me new opportunities. I seek Your wisdom in understanding all the changes that You present. My soul continues to seek You and I continue to hope and wait expectantly. I continue to thank You that Your hand is upon me, encouraging me, and lifting me up. I hold Your hand, praise You, and move forward in this day surrounded by Your love, goodness, and grace. I pray in Jesus' saving name today.

Song Suggestion: Awake My Soul *by* Chris Tomlin feat Lecrae

November 23

Discouragement

When you pass through the waters, I will be with you, and through the rivers, they will not overwhelm you. When you walk through the fire you will not be burned or scorched, nor will the flame kindle upon you.

Isaiah 43:2 (Amp)

Father God,

I like to tell myself that everything in my life will go easy and well for me because I follow You. However, You have long taught us that times of trouble and stress will follow us all our lives. Even though I will have troubles, You say that I will overcome them. I sit quietly in Your holy Presence this morning and I put myself in Your hands. I accept Your help. I will think encouraging thoughts such as: "God, You are holding me, I will not be overwhelmed", "When I walk through the fire, God, You are my protector and I will not be burned", "I will get through this difficult time because You are faithful and I can trust that You are getting me through this", "With You, God, all things are possible." I thank You for being with me, for holding me up and giving me strength, resilience, and grit. I pray with deep, profound gratitude in Jesus' saving name.

Song Suggestion: Another in the Fire *by* Hillsong United

God's Love

Know, recognize and understand therefore that the Lord your God, He is God, the faithful God, Who keeps covenant and steadfast love and mercy with those who love Him and keep His commandments, to a thousand generations.

Deuteronomy 7:9 (Amp)

God, my Father,

I sit quietly with You today, the one true God, and think about how great Your love is. Where would I be without it? It is You Who gives me all I need. It is You Who protects me, comforts me, blesses me, and provides for me. Today I am profoundly grateful for Your deep, faithful, unrelenting, unshakeable love. I am breathing in Your love, and I am putting my Spirit in Your hands. I am giving You my love in return. I am keeping Your commandments and trying my best to live my life on Your terms because I want to honor You. I want to return the love and mercy that You have freely given. I want Your love and mercy to continue in my family for generations. In this moment, I receive Your love and mercy with open hands. I give You praise and thanksgiving from deep within me. I can never praise You or thank You enough. In Jesus' name I pray.

Song Suggestion: God Really Loves Us *by* Crowder, Dante Bowe feat. Maverick City Music

Hope

My soul, wait only upon God and silently submit to Him; for my hope and expectation are from Him. He only is my Rock and my Salvation; He is my Defense and my Fortress, I shall not be moved.

Psalm 62:5-6 (Amp)

Father God,

I come to You this morning quieting myself - my mind, my racing thoughts, and my soul. I come to silently submit my hopes and dreams along with my life to You. I put it all in Your hands. I believe and hope for You to make my path clear. I believe that You will create pathways for me so that I reach my hopes and dreams as well as inspire me to do Your will simultaneously. Only You can make miracles like that happen! I know that there will be 'bumps in the road' but I have a hopeful expectation that You will be with me, giving me the determination to keep going. You are the rock which I am building my life and dreams on. You are my defense and my fortress, protecting me as I journey on. All my hope is in You, Father, Spirit, Jesus. Thank You for giving me hope and being my hope. I pray all these things in Jesus' stable name.

Song Suggestion: Build a Boat *by* Colton Dixon feat Gabby Barrett

Perseverance

If we endure, we shall also reign with Him. If we deny and disown and reject Him, He will also deny and disown and reject us.

2 Timothy 2:12 (Amp)

Father God,

My prayer today is focused on persistence, endurance, and grit. I ask You to help me live Your way day after day, week after week, month after month. It is not an easy task in the world I live in - it can seem like immorality, anger, and ungodliness is closing in on every side. Help me live as an example of Your ways: help me to be forgiving, to be generous, to be kind and compassionate, to live peacefully, to not be easily angered or offended. Help me use my words to show love and gratitude. Help me keep a good attitude despite the trials that surround me. Help me endure hardships while trusting You. Help me be persistent and determined to glorify You and put You first and leave the outcome up to You. I praise You and thank You as I look forward to reigning with You, forever wrapped totally and completely in Your love. In Jesus' holy name I pray.

Song Suggestion: You've Already Won *by* Shane & Shane

November 27

I am a Child of God

See how very much our Father loves us, for he calls us his children, and that is what we are! But the people who belong to this world don't recognize that we are God's children because they don't know him.

1 John 3:1 (NLT)

Father God,

Thank You for Your incredible love. I let Your love surround my soul in this moment. I welcome Your grace to touch me and to help me understand that I am named, I am called, I am counted as Your child. This knowledge and understanding makes me whole. It sets me apart from the world. I am filled with hope, light, and joy. I bring this hope, this light, this joy with me as I go through my day. I bring your light into the world because I am Your beloved child, and You are my beloved Father and Savior. I pray these prayers with unending gratitude in Jesus' name today.

Song Suggestion: Somebody to You *by* Rachel Lampa

Motivation

The work of each [one] will become [plainly, openly] known (shown for what it is); for the day [of Christ] will disclose and declare it, because it will be revealed with fire, and the fire will test and critically appraise the character and worth of the work each person has done. If the work which any person has built on this Foundation [any product of his efforts whatever] survives [this test], he will get his reward.

1 Corinthians 3:13-14 (Amp)

Father God,

I do not like to think about judgment. I feel I am not worthy, not good enough especially when I think about how holy, pure, and perfect You are and how I am not any of those things. I thank You that You are a Father who looks at my heart. I pray that You will continue to work with me to purify my heart, my mind, my attitudes, my motivation, my thoughts, my words, my behavior - all that I do. I pray for an enlightened passion to do Your will. I pray You will open my eyes to see doors that You open as opportunities to be Your hands and feet in this world. Help me stay motivated and persistent every day. In Jesus' name I pray.

Song Suggestion: Set the World on Fire *by* Britt Nicole

Pray for Others

The LORD *also restored the fortunes of Job when he prayed for his friends, and the* LORD *increased double all that Job had.*

Job 42:10 (NASB)

Father God,

Job had an extremely difficult situation, but he prayed without ceasing. Job even prayed for his friends who were accusing him. You answered Job's prayers. I believe You are a God who listens when we pray, and You care for us. I thank You that You are a God who cares about my concerns, my worries - the trivial things and the important things in my life. This morning, like Job, I bring You my prayers for my family and friends. I pray specifically for … (**Note**: *Communicate names of people that You would like to pray for including for people that You think need God's grace in their lives*). I cast my cares on You Lord. I lay (*names*) at Your feet. I thank You for Your deep affection and love for me and my loved ones. I pray in Jesus' saving name today.

Song Suggestion: The Blessing *by* Kari Jobe

I am… Accepted

Therefore, accept each other just as Christ has accepted you so that God will be given glory.

Romans 15:7 (NLT)

Father God,

Sometimes when I think about myself, I think, *I'm a pretty good person, I have never killed anyone, I don't hurt people on purpose, I bend the rules a little bit, but I don't break any laws, I even help others sometimes.* BUT then I read Your Word. I read about how pure, how holy, how loving, how kind, compassionate, and perfect You are. I think about Jesus who forgave His tormentors as they were killing Him. And I realize how far I am from Your perfect ways. The more I read scripture, the more I recognize that I need constant forgiveness and determination to change many of my ungodly habits and behaviors. Yet, You say I am accepted and welcomed even in my sinful, unfaithful, selfish state of being. Wow! I am accepted as I am! I thank You for Your mercy, for Your generosity, for Your faithfulness to me. Please help me turn things around so that I am growing to be more like You. I am so thankful for this journey where You accept me and help me to grow. I am so thankful that I can give You glory, even though I am far from perfect. I pray all these things in Jesus' name.

Song Suggestion: You Say *by* Lauren Daigle

December 1

Holy, Sovereign God

I am the LORD, and there is no other; there is no God besides Me. I will gird you, though you have not known Me, that they may know from the rising of the sun to its setting that there is none besides Me. I am the LORD and there is no other; I form the light and create darkness, I make peace and create calamity; I, the LORD, do all these things.' "Rain down, you heavens, from above, and let the skies pour down righteousness; let the earth open, let them bring forth salvation, and let righteousness spring up together. I, the LORD, have created it.

Isaiah 45:5-8 (NKJV)

Father God,

I believe You are the one, true, holy sovereign God. There is no other like You. You have created all things. You have formed the light and created darkness. You have made a plan for righteousness. You have planned for salvation. I am humbled by Your greatness and Your creativity. Because of Your plan that included the birth and death of Jesus, I am in Your debt as You have made a way for a lost soul like me to enter into Your family, into Your inheritance, into eternity with all other believers who follow You. As I begin the daily countdown to Christmas, help me remember that You are at the center of the season. It is all about You and Your plan and Your love reaching out to us. I thank You and praise You in this moment for being my holy and sovereign Father. You are my Lord and my light. In Jesus' name I pray.

Song Suggestion: Light of the World *by* Lauren Daigle

December 2

Praise

Give thanks to the Lord, *for He is good; for His faithfulness is everlasting. Then say, "Save us, God of our salvation, and gather us and save us from the nations, to give thanks to Your holy name, and glory in Your praise."*

1 Chronicles 16:34-35 (NASB)

Father God,

You are so good, You have given us salvation and it all begins with Christmas. Even though we are focused on trees, shopping, gift giving, baking, and decorating, I am choosing to pause and focus on the true reason for this season. Your loving kindness has broken through from heaven to earth. Your salvation has come. You are gathering those who believe in You so You can rescue us. Your light is shining on us. Therefore, in all that I do this month, I will do it while giving thanks to You, for You are amazing, generous, and kind. I will do everything to honor You and give You glory. I am giving thanks to Your holy name! I am declaring Your praise! You deserve all my praise and worship. You deserve all the honor and thanksgiving. I pray in our Savior's name, Jesus.

Song Suggestion: Angels from the Realm of Glory *by* Paul Baloche

December 3

Wisdom

But the wisdom from above is first of all pure. It is also peace loving, gentle at all times, and willing to yield to others. It is full of mercy and good deeds. It shows no favoritism and is always sincere.

James 3:17 (NLT)

Father God,

Everything about You is perfect, true, pure, and right. James tells us that Your wisdom is pure, peaceful, gentle, and compassionate. Oh, how I seek Your thoughts right now. I ask for more of Your wisdom along with more of Your peace, Your gentleness, Your compassion. I take this time to think about the gentleness of the baby Jesus. He came to this earth in complete peace. He left His kingship in heaven to be with us on earth. He did not come in luxury but came to be with carpenters and shepherds. This turns our worldly wisdom upside down and shows me that I need Your wisdom more than anything else. Let Your light of Christmas shine on me and through me this season. I pray this prayer in Jesus' name.

Song Suggestion: Major Throne *by* Phil Wickham

December 4

Forgiven

Let the wicked change their ways and banish the very thought of doing wrong. Let them turn to the LORD that he may have mercy on them. Yes, turn to our God, for he will forgive generously.

Isaiah 55:7 (NLT)

Father God,

I come to You today admitting that I have unrighteous thoughts and that I do not act in righteous ways consistently. I am acknowledging my mistakes, and I am sorry for doing things my way. I am sorry for sinning against You. I turn to You for forgiveness, mercy, and renewal. You are my compassionate King whose mercies are new every morning. I thank You for Your forgiveness. I thank You for Your kindness and gentleness. I thank You that You do not hold grudges or condemn me. Jesus, as we begin to celebrate the season of Christmas, this is why You came. You came so I could be forgiven. I am in awe of Your birth and Your life where You show me the love of our Father. I thank You for the gifts that You have given and continue to give. In Jesus' name I pray today.

Song Suggestion: Hope Has a Name *by* Kristian Stanfill

Open Ears

Jesus replied, "I have already told you, and you don't believe me. The proof is the work I do in my Father's name. But you don't believe me because you are not my sheep. My sheep listen to my voice; I know them, and they follow me.

John 10:25-27 (NLT)

Father God,

As I get ready to celebrate Your birth, I am thankful that You have come to save me. I am thankful that You know me and count me as one of Your sheep. I am taking time to listen to Your voice today.

I am following You today and always. Open my ears to hear You. I am opening my soul to You so I can be closer to You more than ever. Help me be more willing to follow You, follow You right into eternity where we will be together surrounded by Your light, Your love, Your peace, Your joy. Every day will be like Christmas! Thank You to my Lord, my guide, my Shepherd. I pray in Jesus' name today.

Song Suggestion: I Still Believe in Christmas *by* Anne Wilson

December 6

Joy

"If you keep My commandments, you will abide in My love, just as I have kept My Father's commandments and abide in His love. These things I have spoken to you, that My joy may remain in you, and that your joy may be full.

John 15:10-11 (NKJV)

Father God,

Thank You for giving me the recipe for joy. If I live my life Your way, following Your example, then I will have a full, joyful life. Help me to live my life centered on You and Your teachings. Empower me to see things through Your eyes. As I celebrate the season of Christmas, I am reminded that the undercurrent of the season is joy, joy that the promised Messiah has come, joy that God has come to be with us. And above all, Jesus brings joy to me today because He has given me forgiveness and salvation. Now I live in deep gratitude for the best gift of all: the very first Christmas when the Father sent His Son to come to show his deep, overwhelming, pure love. I choose to focus on this love and joy so I can genuinely enjoy this Christmas season. I pray this joyful and grateful prayer in Jesus' name today.

Song Suggestion: Joy to the World (Joyful, Joyful) *by* Phil Wickham

Love God/Love Others

Beloved, if God so loved us, we also ought to love one another. No one has ever seen God; if we love one another, God remains in us, and His love is perfected in us.

1 John 4:11-12 (NASB)

God, my Father,

You are a 'full circle' God. You love me and You want me to love others. I am deeply thankful for Your love. I ask You to continue to teach me and show me specific ways that I can love and help others. You have been kind to me, help me to be kind to others. You are generous to me, help me to be generous to others. You are patient with me, help me to be patient with others. You are compassionate and merciful to me, help me to be compassionate and merciful to others. Of course, ample opportunities abound at Christmas time to be all these things. With Your help, I can continue to show my love to You and to others now, and well after the Christmas season has passed. Remind me to shine the love and light of Christmas all through the year! Thank You for leading me every day. I pray this is Jesus' holy name.

Song Suggestion: O Holy Night *by* Martina McBride

Names of God

Father of Lights

Do not be deceived, my beloved brethren. Every good gift and every perfect gift is from above, and comes down from the Father of lights, with whom there is no variation or shadow of turning.

James 1:16-17 (NKJV)

Father God,

I thank You and praise You today for every good gift, every perfect gift is directly from You. I take time to think about this. I think about all the blessings in my life… (**Note**: *Communicate to God the blessings that come to mind*). I think about the ultimate gift that You have given: The gift of Your only Son. I think about this beautiful season where the world is brightened by this gift. The Christmas season is also brightened by light.

Lights on houses, lights on trees, lights shining in the windows. You sent a star that lit up the night Jesus was born. You are the Father of light, You created light. Your light drives out the darkness. There is no darkness, not even a shadow in You or around You. I am in awe of my God, my Father. I worship and praise You as the Father of light and of all goodness. In Jesus' name I pray.

Song Suggestion: Christmas Offering *by* Casting Crowns

December 9

Jesus

For unto us a Child is born, Unto us a Son is given; and the government will be upon His shoulder. And His name will be called Wonderful, Counselor, Mighty God, Everlasting Father, Prince of Peace.

Isaiah 9:6 (NKJV)

Jesus,

You came to this world to give me salvation, life, peace, joy, strength, love. You are God's only Son. Our heavenly Father gave You to this world so that we could have an abundant, spiritual life. Right now, I bow down and declare that I am thankful to You, Jesus. I know that Your love is shining on me right here in this moment. May your love for me spill out and shine all around. May You be glorified and lifted high. I believe You were the child that Isaiah foretold about hundreds of years* before You came. I believe You are the Son that was given. I believe You are my Wonderful Counselor, my Mighty God, my Everlasting Father, and the Prince of Peace. I worship at Your feet in this moment with deep gratitude, awe, and praise. In Jesus' name I pray.

*(Isaiah the prophet lived in the year 740 B.C.)

Song Suggestion: Names *by* Elevation Worship

Eternity

"When the Son of Man comes in His glory, and all the holy angels with Him, then He will sit on the throne of His glory. "All the nations will be gathered before Him, and He will separate them one from another, as a shepherd divides his sheep from the goats. And He will set the sheep on His right hand, but the goats on the left. Then the King will say to those on His right hand, 'Come, you blessed of My Father, inherit the kingdom prepared for you from the foundation of the world:

Matthew 25:31-34 (NKJV)

Jesus,

When You came into this world, the holy angels came to announce Your birth to the shepherds who were caring for their sheep in the dark night. We read in today's scripture that when You come back once more, the angels will come with you again. Father God, I am thankful that You have made a plan for me, for all of us. You gave us the gift of Jesus. Thank You for giving us a choice to believe and to follow Jesus as sheep follow a shepherd. Thank You for giving us instructions on how to do this by loving You wholeheartedly and loving others with compassion, kindness, mercy, and action. Help me to do these things more consistently. I thank You that I can look forward to inheriting the kingdom that You have prepared - an eternity with You, enveloped in Your love. I eagerly anticipate when

You send Jesus back again to take me home to be with You. In Jesus' name I pray today.

Song Suggestion: Because of Bethlehem *by* Matthew West

December 11

Believe

She will bear a Son, and you shall call His name Jesus [the Greek form of the Hebrew Joshua, which means Savior], for He will save His people from their sins [that is, prevent them from failing and missing the true end and scope of life, which is God]. All this took place that it might be fulfilled which the Lord had spoken through the prophet. Behold, the virgin shall become pregnant and give birth to a Son, and they shall call His name Emmanuel- which when translated, means, God with us.

Matthew 1:21-23 (Amp)

Jesus,

I believe You were born of the Holy Spirit to Mary and Joseph. I believe You are the Son of God and the Son of Man. I believe You were sent by God, our Father, and willingly came from heaven to earth to save us who believe and follow You. As Christmas approaches and we celebrate Your birth, I vow that I will lean into You, the God of wonders, the God of miracles. I will lean into Your light, Your love, Your peace, and Your joy. I will purposefully remember that You came to save, to show the love of the Father. I will intentionally join You to share Your light, to share Your love with others today, this season, and all my days. I join the heavenly angels saying glory to God in the Highest. Glory to God, our Emmanuel. In Jesus' name I pray today.

Song Suggestion: O What a King *by* Katie Nichole

Peace

I listen carefully to what God the LORD is saying for he speaks peace to his faithful people. But let them not return to their foolish ways. Surely his salvation is near to those who fear him, so our land will be filled with his glory. Unfailing love and truth have met together. Righteousness and peace have kissed!

Psalm 85:8-10 (NLT)

Father God,

I am listening to You this morning. I intentionally quiet my soul and mind. I meditate on Your way, where Your unfailing love and truth have come together. I think of the baby Jesus this way: a miracle where righteousness and peace have been created in a human form. Father and Jesus, thank You for bringing salvation to the world. Help me to stay on Your path, walking with You each day. I want to live my life with You and for You - I do not want to drift away. I want to meditate on Your steadfast love, on Your truth, on Your faithfulness, Your righteousness, and Your peace. It is my prayer that You will continue to teach me and let me experience Your amazing peace. You are such an awesome, amazing God. I put my whole self (body, mind, and spirit) in Your hands today and always. I pray this prayer in Jesus' name today.

Song Suggestion: Glory (Let There Be Peace) *by* Matt Maher

God's Will

For this reason we also, since the day we heard it, do not cease to pray for you, and to ask that you may be filled with the knowledge of His will in all wisdom and spiritual understanding; that you may walk worthy of the Lord, fully pleasing Him, being fruitful in every good work and increasing in the knowledge of God;

Colossians 1:9-10 (NKJV)

Father God,

I greet You with thanksgiving and praise today. I pray this same prayer that Paul prayed over his friends. I am asking You to fill me and my family with the knowledge of Your will. Let Your spiritual wisdom reign over us so that we can live each day with Your grace and Your love flowing through us. Help us to align our purposes with Your purposes.

Empower us to understand what to do in the many circumstances that come our way each day. Guide us to make decisions about what we say and what we do that will reflect You in all Your goodness and light. Help us to be fruitful and not shy away from any good work that You nudge us to do. It does seem easier to do Your will at this time of the year but help us to continue all year long. Help us, help us to do Your will. I pray in Jesus' name.

Song Suggestion: My Soul Magnifies the Lord *by* Chris Tomlin

Thoughts/Mindset

Let not mercy and kindness [shutting out all hatred and selfishness] and truth [shutting out all deliberate hypocrisy or falsehood] forsake you; bind them about your neck, write them upon the tablet of your heart.

Proverbs 3:3 (Amp)

Father God,

Thank You for the freedom You have given me. Thank You for Your instructions - for teaching me the absolute best ways to live! It seems that this time of year opens the world up to Your truth, Your kindness, and Your mindset of love. Many people are more joyful and compassionate. This morning, I meditate on all these good, positive emotions and I recognize that they come directly from You. Today I am imprinting Your mercy, kindness, and truth to my mind and my heart so that I can live in a way that is more reflective of You. I ask the Holy Spirit to help me with this endeavor. I thank You, Jesus, for this amazing season where my thoughts and attitudes are somehow transformed. I give You all the glory and honor as we focus our thoughts and minds on Your birth. I pray with deep gratitude and awe in Jesus, our Savior's name.

Song Suggestion: Giving Christmas Away *by* Tasha Layton

December 15

The Presence of God

Surely the [uncompromisingly] righteous shall give thanks to Your name; the upright shall dwell in Your presence (before Your very face).

Psalm 140:13 (Amp)

Jesus,

Thank You for covering me in Your righteousness. I am made righteous by Your birth, Your death, and resurrection. I take time to quiet myself and be thankful in this moment. I close my eyes and lift my hands to You to send You my heartfelt gratitude for this perfect and selfless gift. I will thank You forever and ever. I will dwell in Your Presence all through my days as best as I can. I thank You repeatedly for Your birth, Your good news of salvation and for Your overwhelming love, mercy, and friendship. I thank You continually for the blessings that are poured on us at Christmas time. And I thank You that I am walking by Your side every day. In Jesus' name I pray today.

Song Suggestion: Thankful *by* Josh Groban

December 16

Trust God

Now when they had departed, behold, an angel of the Lord appeared to Joseph in a dream, saying, "Arise, take the young Child and His mother, flee to Egypt, and stay there until I bring you word; for Herod will seek the young Child to destroy Him." When he arose, he took the young Child and His mother by night and departed for Egypt,

Matthew 2:13-14 (NKJV)

Father God,

I thank You for the Scriptures that were written so long ago. As I read the story about the birth of Jesus, I can see how Mary and Joseph truly trusted in and put their hope in You. They obeyed You at a moment's notice and put their lives in Your hands. Help me to learn from Mary and Joseph. Guide me to surrender to You and trust You when I do not always understand. Empower me to trust You when hard things come. I know that You are with me, and You will help me through life's circumstances. I put myself in Your hands now, with gratitude for all I have and all You are doing in my life. I trust You more consistently because You are trustworthy and faithful. I pray In Jesus' holy name.

Song Suggestion: Be Born in Me (Mary) *by* Francesca Battistelli

December 17

Forgiving

If you forgive anyone's sins, they are forgiven. If you do not forgive them, they are not forgiven."

John 20:23 (NLT)

Father God,

Did Mary and Joseph forgive the innkeeper for not finding them a room when it was time for the birth of Jesus? There is no record of any "feelings" of anger/resentment on their part. If I were in that situation, could I forgive so easily? Now that I know that You call me to forgive others, no matter what my feelings are, I am deciding to forgive others who anger me, who hurt me, who disappoint me, who oppose me. I will forgive others who appear to think only of themselves and are not kind, considerate, or compassionate.

This is a choice and I choose to obey You. Christmas reminds us of all Jesus' has done and that His ways are the best ways. Like Jesus did, I choose love. I choose light. I choose life. I choose obedience. I believe You will help me (as I will need it). I love You and praise You Father. Thank You for sending Jesus to give me forgiveness. I pray in Jesus' name.

Song Suggestion: Christmas Changes Everything *by* Josh Wilson

My Words

For the Scriptures say, "If you want to enjoy life and see many happy days, keep your tongue from speaking evil and your lips from telling lies. Turn away from evil and do good. Search for peace, and work to maintain it.

1 Peter 3:10-11 (NLT)

God, my Father,

I want to enjoy my life and see good days! Thank You for teaching me and helping me see that learning Your ways will help me be more content. Your Word tells me that my joy is tied to what I say. With Your guidance, I will continue to work on saying positive, uplifting, and helpful things to myself and others. I will lean on You when I need help. It is easy to say I will speak joyfully when I am here with You: alone and peaceful. It can be easier at this time of the year with "Joy to the World" and "Holly Jolly Christmas" tunes playing in the background. It gets difficult the minute I get annoyed or offended. Right now, I am thinking about how I can use my words to bless others, and how I can pursue peace with my words. Thank You for giving me the chance to have an abundant, full, merry life. You are truly a God of blessings. In Jesus' name I pray.

Song Suggestion: The Joy (Live) *by* The Belonging Co

December 19

Anxiety

"So don't worry about these things, saying, 'What will we eat? What will we drink?" What will we wear?' These things dominate the thoughts of unbelievers, but your heavenly Father already knows all your needs. Seek the Kingdom of God above all else, and live righteously, and he will give you everything you need. So don't worry about tomorrow, for tomorrow will bring its own worries. Today's trouble is enough for today.

Matthew 6:31-34 (NLT)

Father God,

Christmas time tends to make my anxieties worse - there are financial issues, relationship issues, demanding schedules. However, I am grateful that as holy and sovereign as You are, You are still aware of my needs. I can think back and remember the many times that You have answered my prayers. I can remember the Christmas' of the past and I can see that You were enough. I am so thankful that You hear me, You see me and You know me. Jesus, You want me to put You first - in all aspects of my life. It seems a bit easier to do at Christmas time, but I want to put You first in my thoughts, in my decisions, in all areas of my life even after the feelings of Christmas subside. As I do this, I will not need to be anxious or worried because You will give me everything I need. Teach me to depend on You as I seek You every day. I take some quiet, restful breaths in this moment. I breathe in Your peaceful, tranquil thoughts. I breathe out all worries, anxieties, and tensions. I give them to You. I know that You are my rock, my shield, and my strength. I pray this prayer with a deeply grateful heart, in Jesus' name.

Song Suggestion: The Hope of Christmas *by* Matthew West

Thankful

"And you, my little son, will be called the prophet of the Most High, because you will prepare the way for the Lord. You will tell his people how to find salvation through forgiveness of their sins. Because of God's tender mercy, the morning light from heaven is about to break upon us, to give light to those who sit in darkness and in the shadow of death, and to guide us to the path of peace."

Luke 1:76-79 (NLT)

Father God,

Thank You for the written history and the gospels that give us information about the birth of Jesus. Thank You for the story of John the Baptist who came to 'prepare the way for the Lord.' Thank You for telling us how to find salvation and how to be forgiven from our sins. Thank You for Your tender mercy, for sending Jesus - 'the morning light from heaven.' In this moment, just days before Christmas, I take time to celebrate that the 'morning light from heaven is about to break upon us.' I celebrate that You 'give us light and that we are no longer in darkness or in the shadow of death.' You have sent us a guide to help us find the path of peace. You have done all of this for us, in Your mercy and Your love. I am sending my deep gratitude for all these blessings. I am deeply grateful for the true history and meaning of Christmas. I am thankful for Your good plan for me and all of humankind. I am profoundly grateful for the birth of my Savior, Jesus. In Jesus' name I pray this prayer.

Song Suggestion: Born On That Day *by* Matt Maher

December 21

Prayer

When they saw the star, they were thrilled with ecstatic joy. And on going into the house, they saw the Child with Mary His mother, and they fell down and worshiped Him. Then opening their treasure bags, they presented to Him gifts-gold and frankincense and myrrh. And receiving an answer to their asking, they were divinely instructed and warned in a dream not to go back to Herod; so they departed to their own country by a different way.

Matthew 2:10-12 (Amp)

Father God,

Thank You for answering prayers. I see right in the Christmas story that the wise men received an 'answer to their asking' and You divinely guided them. I thank You that You still hear prayers. I ask that You continue to divinely guide me and instruct me just as You did to the wisemen all those years ago. I am grateful as I celebrate this beautiful season that I can join the wisemen in worshiping You as my King. Although I do not have gold, frankincense, and myrrh, I do give You my worship, my praise, my thanksgiving, and my helping hands for You to use as my gift today. I pray this prayer in Jesus' name today.

Song Suggestion: The Night Before Christmas *by* Brandon Heath

December 22

Seek God

When the angels went away from them into heaven, the shepherds said one to another, let us go over to Bethlehem and see this thing (saying) that has come to pass, which the Lord has made known to us. So they went with haste and (by searching) found Mary and Joseph, and the Baby lying in a manger.

Luke 2:15-16 (Amp)

Father God,

As we approach the celebration of Jesus' birth, I want to let go of everything and seek You like the Shepherds did at Your birth. Help me to open my mind and heart to You. Help me to open myself to the love of You, my Father, who sent Your only Son to us. Help me to open myself to the wonder of Jesus, leaving His home in heaven to be born in a humble manger. Help me open myself to the fullness of the good news that a Savior has come to save me because I cannot save myself. Open my eyes and heart to the wonder and love of this beautiful gift that the shepherds found: Jesus. Let me continue my life's journey with persistent searching for You, and seeking You, Father, Spirit, and Jesus. I pray in Jesus' name.

Song Suggestion: Noel *by* Lauren Daigle

Discouragement

At that time there was a man in Jerusalem named Simeon. He was righteous and devout and was eagerly waiting for the Messiah to come and rescue Israel. The Holy Spirit was upon him and had revealed to him that he would not die until he had seen the Lord's Messiah. That day the Spirit led him to the Temple. So when Mary and Joseph came to present the baby Jesus to the Lord as the law required, Simeon was there. He took the child in his arms and praised God, saying, "Sovereign Lord, now let your servant die in peace, as you have promised. I have seen your salvation, which you have prepared for all people. He is a light to reveal God to the nations, and he is the glory of your people Israel."

Luke 2:25-32 (NLT)

Father God,

As everyone is celebrating this time of year with festive activities, I sometimes experience negative feelings. I have had difficult and challenging times this past year and I am feeling disappointment and discouragement. Today as I read about Simeon, I can connect with him because Simeon is someone who must have had discouraging feelings. He had waited so long and not seen his dream come to pass. I also read that Simeon continued to 'eagerly wait.' As I sit in Your Presence this morning, help me change my discouragement to hope. Help me know that good things have already come with the birth of Jesus and all the promises that Jesus brings. Help me know that I can eagerly wait and hope for the good things that You have planned for me. Help me change my thinking and my attitude. Fill me with Your thoughts, Your hopes, Your light. You are the hope of the world, and You are my hope. In Jesus' name I pray today.

Song Suggestion: Hope Was Born This Night *by* Sidewalk Prophets

God's Love

And suddenly there was with the angel a multitude of the heavenly host praising God and saying: "Glory to God in the highest, and on earth peace, goodwill toward men!"

Luke 2:13-14 (NKJV)

Father God,

Tonight, we celebrate a very holy night. It was so holy that a multitude of angels came to announce God's gift of love. Although people on earth, then and now, do not consistently live with peace or goodwill in their hearts, You Father, sent Your peace and Your goodwill to us anyway. I can see Your pattern: You give to us though we are undeserving. You give Your love when we are unloving. You give us Your hope though we turn away in despair. You give Your peace even though we create stress, anxiety, and chaos. In this moment, I sit quietly with You, and I remember the multitude of angels declaring Your glory, Your goodwill, Your peace, and I join them in praising You for all Your goodness, for all Your gifts. I say, "Glory to You Father, Glory to You Jesus and Glory to You, Holy Spirit." "Glory to God in the Highest" I declare from my heart to Yours on this very special day. I pray in Jesus' our Savior's name.

Song Suggestion: Glory in the Highest *by* Chris Tomlin

Hope/Christmas

And behold, an angel of the Lord stood before them, and the glory of the Lord shone around them, and they were greatly afraid, then the angel said to them, "Do not be afraid, for behold, I bring you good tidings of great joy which will be to all people. For there is born to you this day in the city of David a Savior, who is Christ the Lord. And this will be the sign to you: You will find a Babe wrapped in swaddling cloths, lying in a manger."

Luke 2:9-12 (NKJV)

Father God,

You gave us the most precious of all gifts, the gift of Your only Son. His birth was announced as 'good tidings of great joy.' Christmas is often known as 'the most wonderful time of the year.' I intentionally remember that this is true because of the love You have shown, and the joy and hope that Your love brings into my life not only at Christmas but every day. I celebrate this love, joy, and hope with You now. I celebrate the birth of Christ, my Lord. I am filled with deep gratitude and awe for this good news, for this great love. Help me share Your great love, joy, and hope with all whom I meet, not just today but all through the year. And before the festivities begin, I take some quiet time with You to say, "Thank You for the best gift ever given and to say Merry Christmas Father, Jesus, and Holy Spirit." I pray with joy in Jesus' name today.

Song Suggestion: Away in a Manger *by* Phil Wickham

December 26

Perseverance

Because you have obeyed my command to persevere, I will protect you from the great time of testing that will come upon the whole world to test those who belong to this world. I am coming soon. Hold on to what you have, so that no one will take away your crown.

Revelation:10-11 (NLT)

Father God,

We have just celebrated the birth of our Lord, our Savior - Your Son Who came to save us, not condemn us; Your son who came to give us a choice to follow Him and have a spiritually abundant life filled with joy, peace, hope, and love as we choose to live Your way - the best way. All throughout Your Word, You tell us that Jesus is coming back.

Help me keep Your Christmas Spirit close to me - the Spirit of life and all things good, pure, noble, and excellent. Help me keep my faith in You flourishing so that I will be ready for You when You come again. Thank You for protecting me and continuing to protect me. I will persevere and continue to praise Your name forever. I continue to pray, "Glory in the highest". In Jesus name I pray.

Song Suggestion: He Shall Reign Forever More *by* Chris Tomlin

December 27

I am a Child of God

Dear friends, we are already God's children, but he has not yet shown us what we will be like when Christ appears. But we do know that we will be like him, for we will see him as he really is.

1 John 3:2 (NLT)

Father God and Jesus,

We have just celebrated Your birth and the good news that You brought to the world. Your life changed the entire world in so many ways, more than I can comprehend. Now, I wait for You to come again. I am waiting for You, remembering that every day I live, I am living as Your child. I am living for You, waiting with expectant hope that all will be made right. Because I am Your child, I will live in such a way as to honor You. I believe You are with me, cheering me on, helping me, picking me up when I falter. I believe You are for me. I thank You for choosing me to be Your child. I thank You for having a plan for me. I thank You that someday, I will see You as You really are - in all Your glory. I praise You as I pray this prayer in Jesus' name today.

Song Suggestion: You Changed My Name *by* Matthew West

Motivation

Whatever may be your task, work at it heartily (from the soul), as [something done] for the Lord and not for men, knowing [with all certainty] that it is from the Lord [and not from men] that you will receive the inheritance which is your [real] reward. [The One Whom] you are actually serving [is] the Lord Christ (the Messiah).

Colossians 3:23-24 (Amp)

Father God,

Let this scripture be my prayer every day! Help me to remember that everything I do, I can purposefully do it for You! When I am at home, I will dedicate my tasks (the never-ending dishes and laundry, the vacuuming, the outdoor chores.) as a service to You. When I go to work, I will do my best, not wasting time, not complaining, not spending time on my phone. I will have integrity and I will do my job with excellence as I will be doing it as a service to You. I pray today that Your Holy Spirit will infuse a godly spirit and attitude in me every day. Help me, help me, Lord, for I want to live for You. In Jesus' name I pray.

Song Suggestion: How Many Kings *by* Downhere

December 29

Pray for Others

For the grace of God that brings salvation has appeared to all men,

Titus 2:11 (NKJV)

Father God,

You have come to this world to give us salvation. You have come to give us grace even though we do not deserve it. I am thankful that You have come. As the days of Christmas, when we celebrate the birth of Your Son, come to a close, I continue my journey to follow You more closely. But for many other people, Jesus' birth is forgotten, and life goes on without You in it. This morning, I am praying for others who do not know Your life changing love. Specifically, I pray for… (**Note**: *Communicate to God names of people who come to mind*). I pray that those I pray for will know the truth of Your birth and will internalize the reason for Your coming. I pray that the spirit of Christmas will continue to open the hearts and minds of those who may believe but do not have a meaningful, growing relationship with You. As we come close to the end of this year, my prayer is that You crack open our hearts a little more so we can all feel Your Presence with more clarity. In Jesus' name I pray today.

Song Suggestion: By Your Grace *by* Cody Johnson

I am… Chosen and Special

But you are not like that, for you are a chosen people. You are royal priests, a holy nation, God's very own possession. As a result, you can show others the goodness of God, for he called you out of the darkness into his wonderful light.

1 Peter 2:9 (NLT)

Father God,

I am chosen, I am special, I am Your possession. I am grateful for the grace and mercy that You have shown me. You are a perfect, holy God and I am a sinner. Despite that, You have called me into Your light and that is where I want to stay. I declare that You are an excellent, perfect Father. I declare that You have done wonderful things for me. I declare that You have brought me out of darkness into light. Therefore, I have the opportunity to show all those around me Your goodness. I am forever grateful that I am chosen and special because of YOU. I pray in deep gratitude and praise in Jesus' name.

Song Suggestion: Made for More *by* Josh Baldwin

I Will...

Do to others whatever you would like them to do to you. This is the essence of all that is taught in the law and the prophets.

Matthew 7:12 (NLT)

Father God,

Today I sit quietly and think about all I have learned about You this past year. I love the time that we have spent quietly together. I am deeply grateful for the life-changing impact You have made in my life. In today's scripture, I see that "The Golden Rule" that I have heard throughout my life comes right from Jesus. As I begin a new year, I think about this life altering teaching. I think about how living this way intentionally every day will continue to change my life. I desire to follow You and to obey Jesus' teaching. I will do my best to do to others what I would like them to do to me. I will be kind in all circumstances. I will look for ways to be thoughtful to others. I will be generous. I will be a source of encouragement to others. I will not be a complainer. I will not make excuses. I will not be impatient or rude even when I am having a difficult day. I will act in love. I ask You to help me every day. I pray in Jesus' name on this New Year's Eve.

Song Suggestion: And Now My Lifesong Sings *by* Casting Crowns

ACKNOWLEDGEMENTS

First and foremost, I am so very thankful for my husband. Thank you, Steve, for all the times you shut the TV off, lowered the phone volume, and good naturedly kept things quiet so I could write this devotional in our shared space. You are a huge support for me, a steady source of encouragement. You are my one true love and a gift from God.

Thank you, Chris and Wayne Glogowski, for stepping out of your comfort zone and inviting Steve and me to a non- denominational church all those years ago.

Thank you, Peggy Moorehouse, not only for being such a wonderful friend, but also for your direction and encouragement.

And a special shout out to my most excited supporter, my mother-in-law, Marilyn Ullmann. Your interest and enthusiasm have meant so much to me.

I would also like to take this opportunity to thank my D.E.A.P. friends. D.E.A.P. (Drop Everything And Pray) is derivative of an education practice called DEAR time (Drop Everything And Read). A group of coworkers and I met once a month (before I retired) to pray together. I want to thank all the participants of that group and especially Rowena Rao and Debbie Alexander for their early encouragement and later, Amy Drejas for her encouragement in the last years. I believe that without this successful public prayer experience, I could not have written this devotional.

I have had many influences that helped me build my faith which has given me a foundation which this devotional is built on. My very first influence occurred when I found a Christian radio station and started to listen to Dr. David Jeremiah on the drive to work and Charles Stanley (In Touch Radio Ministries) on the way home from work. Wow. They taught about the Bible and Christianity in a whole new way than I had ever heard. I somehow came across Joyce Meyer Ministries on TV. Joyce turned my whole perception of religion and how I was living upside down. I still watch Joyce Meyer on my iPad and TV and she is still teaching me to this day. I also discovered K-LOVE and Air1 Christian radio which has been a source of influence as well. I have been a self-engaged learner and have also been impacted by Andy Stanley (North Point Church), Craig Groeschel (Life.Church), Rick Warren (author of Purpose Driven Life and pastor of Saddleback Church). I am also indebted to the teachings and messages from Dr. Rex Keener, my pastor for the past 12 years (Grace Fellowship in Latham, NY) and Chad Bryan (previous youth pastor of Halfmoon Campus of Grace Fellowship) who taught me that it is ok to be my free-spirited self while volunteering, teaching and mentoring high school students. These teachers have paved the way for my faith and for this book. All these influences have helped me to learn about God's wisdom, grace, salvation (just to name a few) but more importantly have given me direct instruction on how to apply God's Word in my life. I have learned that it is not about religious rules or a checklist of things to do. It is about inviting God into Your life and pursuing a lifelong relationship with Him at the center of it all.